M000005303

The 'Haunts' of
ROBIN
HOOD

The 'Haunts' of ROBIN HOOD

Jill Armitage

TEMPUS

Frontispiece: Where will we find the ghost of Robin Hood?

First published 2007

Tempus Publishing Limited
The Mill, Brimscombe Port,
Stroud, Gloucestershire, GL5 2QG
www.tempus-publishing.com

© Jill Armitage, 2007

The right of Jill Armitage to be identified as the Author
of this work has been asserted in accordance with the
Copyrights, Designs and Patents Act 1988.

All rights reserved. No part of this book may be reprinted
or reproduced or utilised in any form or by any electronic,
mechanical or other means, now known or hereafter invented,
including photocopying and recording, or in any information
storage or retrieval system, without the permission in writing
from the Publishers.

British Library Cataloguing in Publication Data.
A catalogue record for this book is available from the British Library.

ISBN 978 0 7524 4331 7

Typesetting and origination by Tempus Publishing Limited.
Printed in Great Britain.

Contents

Adrian, Darius and André
May the spirit of Robin be with you always

I would like to thank Andrea Sloman for inspiring me to write this book, Lady Armitage for permission to tour the Kirklees Estate, Mr B. Wheatley for allowing me to visit Robin Hood's Stable, Mr Will Richards, Blidworth historian, for pointing me in the right direction and Sir Reresby Sitwell for sharing his knowledge and giving his permission to reproduce the photograph of Robin Hood's Bow.

Introduction

'Why are you writing about Robin Hood? Hasn't it all been done a million times before?' people asked while I was researching this book. I used to smile and nod in agreement, then change the subject, and that's not because I didn't want to talk about it, but because no one would believe me if I did. It's only now that *The Haunts of Robin Hood* is finished that I've decided to let you all into the secret.

I was in the middle of writing *Ghost Pets and Spirit Animals* when a psychic informed me that Robin Hood was with me because I was going to write a book about him. 'Oh no I'm not,' I assured her and, without wanting to turn this into a pantomime routine, she replied, 'Oh yes you are.' Now let's face it, a subject like Robin Hood is not the kind of burning issue that automatically sends you rushing to switch on your PC. As a writer, I'm always looking for interesting ideas but as far as I was concerned, the tales of Robin Hood had been done to death. No, that's probably the wrong turn of phrase, because these stories never die. Like old fairy tales, they are traditional, with an enchantment that never fades. That's why romantic films are still being made of them, comic strips pick fragments out of the mosaic and thousands of people visit Sherwood Forest every year.

I was still scoffing at the very idea of it when she informed me that Robin would help me. I laughed rather shakily. 'Will he help me find a publisher too?' Her voice was very serious. 'Robin says that will be no problem at all.' Oh yes! Little did she/he know; finding a publisher who likes your ideas and is looking for just that kind of book at just that time is like finding a pot of gold at the end of a rainbow, but as I was actually contracted to Tempus to write *Ghost Pets and Spirit Animals*, I tentatively asked my editor Emily if she would be interested. I'm sure I sounded like some raving lunatic, but Emily listened patiently.

'So what you are proposing is being the ghost writer – no pun intended – of an autobiography by Robin Hood, 2006?' The idea sounded even more weird and wacky when someone else voiced it. 'Yes.' Emily declined my offer.

Looking back, it now seems like madness, yet, even with the odds stacked against me, I decided to do a bit of research and was soon totally involved in a scenario that was not only producing a book, but a gazetteer of sites that Robin had known. Added to this, I found that lots of the sites were haunted, which added an extra, unexpected element, so I asked my psychic contact if Robin Hood haunted anywhere in particular. She said he did but she wasn't prepared to say where: it was up to me to find him.

With that kind of challenge how could I refuse? I again approached Emily. 'Sorry, we did a Robin Hood book six years ago, and we've just commissioned a book on haunted

A spiritually channelled sketch of Losa, but am I really a reincarnation of Maid Marion's handmaiden?

Nottinghamshire,' she explained, as she rejected the proposal again. So much for having no problem finding a publisher! 'But can I send you a partial?' I wheedled and, unenthusiastically, she agreed. I sent ten pages, she emailed to say she liked it and would be putting it before the publishing committee the following Wednesday. Fortunately, they liked the idea too, and within a week I had a contract, so perhaps Robin was right. Now all I had to do was find him, or rather his ghost.

It wasn't until I was halfway through the book that my contact dropped another bomb shell. Apparently the reason I had become so involved with the research was because I had been there with them – those merrie men. I was the reincarnation of Maid Marion's hand-maiden/companion, and my name was Losa. I felt quite unsteady. It's not every day you're told such news. Apparently Losa had devoted her life to Marion, unlike most of her friends who had disowned her when she went to live with Robin in the Greenwood. Losa had stayed loyal and gone with her. I was told it was Losa who was guiding me to places Robin had known and giving me inspiration for the book. She was also helping me uncover new findings and answers to many old questions.

It's quite an unnerving thought, but I think she has done exactly that because my research has taken me in directions previously never envisaged. So why not come with us on our quest for the ghost of Robin Hood and see who else we encounter on the way? We'll travel through Nottinghamshire, Derbyshire, Yorkshire and touch Staffordshire to discover places mentioned in the early ballads, ancient sites, interesting statues, aged artefacts, geographic features that have been given the outlaw's names, and loads of stories of the ghosts that haunt Robin Hood Country.

Setting the Scene

When the Roman legions began their conquering drives through England, they found a country of vast, impenetrable woodland, choked with seemingly endless dense growth. No one had ventured to carve through it, yet there were some existing ridge-way tracks skirting the major forest areas and it was these that the Romans followed when constructing their roads.

Places like Sherwood Forest remained uncharted and ill-defined. Only wild and uncertain tracks and occasional clearings, known as dales, made it possible for a few diminutive villages to spring up, villages like Sutton, Kirkby, Edwinstowe and Blidworth. The inhabitants of these villages scratched a living from the dry, sandy Sherwood soil and lived on the primitive trades of the forest, as charcoal burners, colliers and woodmen.

England was still predominantly forest at the time of the Norman invasion in 1066, yet things were about to change radically. It was William the Conqueror, governing like a military dictator, who established the term Royal Forest when he claimed around ninety areas where all timber and game was the property of the King, and the Norman aristocracy enjoyed exclusive privilege of the chase.

To uphold these new rules, he imposed a system of fines, taxes and licenses known as Forest Law, maintained by William's henchmen with a severity previously unknown in England. Saxon barons and Churchmen who had previously held land found that the new laws only allowed them the occasional special dispensation; any dogs that were kept had to have three claws from their forefeet removed to prevent them being used for hunting. The punishment for infringement of the forest laws was barbarous: a man could 'answer with his body' – a phrase that encompassed hanging and such mutilation as castration and blinding. Whole villages were starving, yet they were fined as a penalty for the unexplained disappearance of a deer.

However, if an offender could pay, pay he did because England's Kings always tended to be short of money. A substantial fine paid into the royal coffers was far more welcome than a severed hand, so the forest laws spelt money. Many peasants still tried to scratch a living from the land, yet the King sold the best to the Church enabling huge monastic establishments like Newstead Abbey, Rufford Abbey and Welbeck to flourish. The early asceticism of the monastic orders enabled these colonies to subsist almost anywhere and the monk's skills in agriculture led them to redeem the most difficult land. Yet they became greedy and grabbed all the land around, oblivious to the needs of the locals who relied on the forest for their livelihood. This exploitation understandably made the monks very unpopular.

Against this background of unrest and inequality, in the forest theatre of Sherwood, the stage was set for the appearance of the celebrated Robin Hood and his companions to perform their own kind of forest rule.

Above: An early medieval illustration depicting the King hunting in the Royal Forest.

Left: Robin Hood in the Greenwood.

Robin Hood in the Greenwood: the tales of Robin Hood

The history that is written down is not always a true guide to what actually happened in times gone by: in fact, medieval history is an astonishing mass of misrepresentation and blunders. Through the historical sieve, the early chroniclers conserved anything they considered worthy and discarded the rest, and sadly, our hero was thrown on the reject pile. He was never mentioned by early English historians, because in former times history was written by monks who were unwilling to highlight the exploits of an outlaw who poked fun at the uncharitable hypocrisy of the monastic establishments. They couldn't deny it, so they tried to suppress it, yet their efforts were in vain. The peasants needed a hero they could identify with, a man of the time who waged a perpetual war against the powerful Norman barons, defied the unjust laws, ridiculed authority and robbed the rich to feed the poor. It didn't matter to the masses that nothing was written down, because everything that was documented was handwritten in Latin, not the language spoken in the streets, and the majority of people couldn't read anyway.

The balladeers and minstrels, on the other hand, picked up the news wherever they went and passed it on in song. They were the reporters of the day who observed and recorded everyday events with uncanny accuracy. These news carriers were entertainers who related the activities of Robin Hood and his men in rhyme and rhythm. They became the pop songs of the day, soon learnt, easily retained, enthusiastically recalled and sung by the people to ease the pain of daily labour.

With the exploits of Robin Hood, the wandering minstrels had a winning formula. They wove a patchwork of fact and fiction into the contemporary culture of the time, and were constantly seeking a new twist to an old story to add to their repertoire and please an ever-growing audience.

By 1340 the ballads had obviously circulated far and wide because the Scottish historian Fordum wrote in reference to Robin Hood and his men: 'the foolish and vulgar are delighted to hear the jesters and minstrels sing them above all other ballads.' In the *Visions of Pierce Ploughman*, an allegorical poem composed soon after 1360 and generally ascribed to Robert Langeland, the author introduces a drunken secular priest who confessed, 'I can ryms of Robin Hode and Randolf, Earl of Chester, but of our lorde or our lady, I lerne nothyng at all'.

So the legends and stories of Robin and his outlaw band were obviously far older than the first written mention, a collection of stories or fables with the title *The Lytell Geste of Robyn Hode* (the deeds and history of Robin Hood), preserved in the British Museum. These stories, set to music, were told in rhyming verse in the vernacular, the language spoken in the streets, yet each had a strong moralistic tone with a pious conclusion often added at the end. This gives a clue

The tales of Robin and his men spread far and wide. (H. Pyle)

A LYTELL GESTE OF ROBYN HODE.

This ancient legend is printed from the copy of an edition, in 4to. and black letter, by Wynken de Worde, preserved in the public library at Cambridge; compared with, and in some places corrected by, another impression (apparently from the former), likewise in 4to. and black letter, by William Copland; a copy of which is among the late Mr. Garrick's old plays, now in the British Museum. The full title of the first edition is as follows: " Here beginneth a mery geste of Robyn Hode and his meyne, and of the proude sheryfe of Notyngham;" and the printer's colophon runs thus: " Explycit. Kynge Edwarde and Robyn Hode & Lytell Johan, Emprented at London in Flete Strete at the sygne of th Sone, by Wynken de Worde." To Copland's edition is added " a new playe for to be played in Maye games very plesaunte and full of pastyme;" which will be found at large at the end of the volume.

Above left: Title page illustration of William Copeland's edition of the *Lytell Geste of Robin Hood, c.* 1550.

Above right: The first printed stories – the *Lytell Geste of Robyn Hode* engraved after Bewick, from Joseph Ritson's *Robin Hood.*

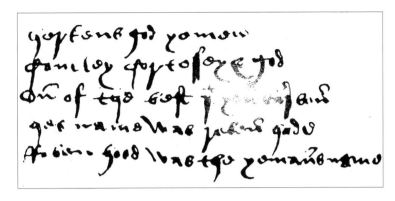

Can you decipher this section from the original manuscript, *Robin Hood and the Potter*? Robin Hood is written at the beginning of the fifth line.

as to who might have written them, because there is every likelihood that they were compiled by some elderly monk to relieve the tedium of monastic life and break the monotony of his meditations. Such a person was Richard Rolle (1290-1349), also known as Richard of Hampole, who wrote poetry on religious and other subjects.

Richard, known as the Hermit of Hampole, was an eremite residing at the nunnery of Hampole, less than a mile from where the action took place at Barnsdale. Richard based his ballads on the places he knew: he could never have envisaged that those early stories would, centuries later, be picked over by learned historians in an attempt to sort out the locations and create a friendly feud between Nottinghamshire and Yorkshire, who both want to claim Robin Hood.

In 1476, William Caxton set up the first printing press in England in the precinct of Westminster Abbey. When his assistant, Wynken de Worde, inherited the business in 1500, he moved the press to a new site beside St Bride's church, Fleet Street. Here he printed school books and cheap editions of popular works. The term 'Chap book' is applied to these small, cheap booklets, which usually consisted of twenty-four pages, sold by peddlers – cheap, chep or chap-men, who also sold broadsheets and ballads.

By this time, a number of Richard Rolle's manuscripts were already well known and had been printed by Wynken de Worde, who was also the first to print the stories of Robin Hood, a further fact to reinforce the belief that Richard also wrote *The Lytell Geste*. From the oral traditions and the early broadsides and chap books, around forty distinct ballads survive, many in multiple versions. These laid down the foundation of a saga that has endured the succeeding centuries and been perpetuated by each generation.

Books, plays, pantomimes, operas, TV, film and big screen productions have continued to embellish and develop the story until Robin Hood has become the most popular and best-known outlaw hero in the world. The legendary halo that has gathered round his name has resulted in a timeless fascination with Robin and his outlaw gang, but who were these people? Were they saints or sinners?

Certain names come readily to mind – Robin Hood was always the leader of his gang of merrie men who had names like Little John, Friar Tuck, Will Scarlet and Allen a Dale. Robin had no obvious female companionship until Elizabethan playwright Anthony Munday introduced Maid Marion, yet with so many men away at the Crusades, there would be no shortage of lonely, frustrated women willing to pick the lock on their chastity belts for a virile outlaw – perhaps not something a monk like Richard Rolle would know about.

So Who was Robin Hood?

Nobleman, yeoman or peasant? Robin Hood has purportedly been all of these, and we will never be sure. Prior to the nineteenth century there was no official register of births or deaths: the only records were judicial or ecclesiastical and were very sketchy at best, particularly as surnames, which were only developed as a means of revealing a person's social standing, were not in general use. Yeoman's surnames like Miller, Baker and Nailor recorded their trade or business activity, in comparison to the peasant who was known only as the son of someone – Johnson, Williamson, Jackson. The aristocracy drew attention to their place of birth, ancestry or estate, and the barons used the name of their earldoms, so unless someone was born into high office, the chances of appearing on record were very remote and allowance must also be made for corrupt spelling.

There is every possibility that the name Robin Hood was a nickname to hide his true identity and protect his family. The name could have been a play on words, robber-in-a-hood, or robber-in-the-wood. In America, the word 'hood' is used to describe a gangster, and 'hobbes-hod' was a generic name for an outlaw or robber in medieval England. Hood could also be a shortened form of hoodlum meaning a good-for-nothing, lawless youth. These all fit the description of our legendary outlaw, so the name Robin Hood certainly points to just one thing – a man living outside the law.

For hundreds of years, historians have picked at a hazy jumble of assorted evidence to try to pin down Robin's existence, status and origins to a specific person, time and place. In the *Geste* and other early ballads, Robin is referred to as Robin of Barnsdale, Sir Walter Scott called him Robin of Loxley and he's generally referred to as Robin of Sherwood.

In 1521 John Major placed Robin against the dates 1160-93 during the reign of Richard the Lionheart, and over the years, this has been accepted by most people. The concept that Robin was an unjustly disinherited earl, driven from his estates and forced to live as an outlaw alongside the peasants, added to the pastoral charm of the tales yet he would have had status because amongst the outlaws he was their master and always addressed so; in the outlaw camp, Robin reigned like an independent sovereign. When Robin was taken prisoner by the Sheriff, he couldn't string him up like a common criminal: in fact, he couldn't do anything until he had the permission of the King.

Elizabethan playwright Anthony Munday published two plays on the life of Robin Hood proclaiming him the Earl of Huntington. A century later, William Stukeley attempted to authenticate the Huntington theme by tracing Robin's ancestry, and, in 1746, he produced a family tree showing that the Earl of Huntington, during the reign of Richard I, had the name Robert Fitz Othe. It's very easy to modify the name Robert Fitz Othe to Robin Hood. Many

Roberts were called Robin, and the name Fitz was given to the illegitimate son of a nobleman, showing that royal blood flowed through their veins. It was straightforward to drop the name Fitz and be known simply as Robin Othe.

Across the country there were so many local dialects that it was almost impossible for a word to sound the same in any two, so Othe could be pronounced Uth. There was no standardization of spelling prior to the publication of Samuel Johnson's *Dictionary* in 1755, so a name or word could be spelt in a large variety of ways. What looked strange to the eye might be more familiar to the ear. The 'th' sound in Middle English was often written as a letter 'D', making Othe into Ode, Oda or Odo (all pronounced like odour), so it is quite possible that this is a descendent of the Bishop Odo, William the Conqueror's half brother who died in 1097 and was known to have sired many illegitimate children.

In 1795, the antiquarian Joseph Ritson was so convinced of Robin Hood's historicality that he attempted a biography, culminating in the *Life of Robin Hood*, yet people still say that Robin and his men have been forged by imaginative ballad makers rather than by factual circumstances. The lack of early information and failure to give our hero an identity other than Robin Hood is, to some, an indication that no such person actually existed except in fantasy, but others still continue to try to identify the man behind the name. Sadly, the sparse information we have has been mulled over, changed and distorted over the centuries, so we will never know for sure. Let's just agree with one writer who said: 'If Robin hadn't existed it would have been necessary to invent him.'

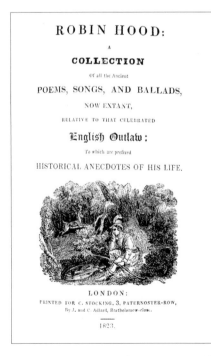

Above left: A collection of poems, songs and ballads; from the frontispiece of Joseph Ritson's *Robin Hood, c.* 1823.

Above right: A fine wooden carving of Robin Hood made from Sherwood oak.

Maid Marion

It is unlikely that the prefix 'maid' indicated that Marion was a serving wench; it's more likely that 'maid' is a shortened form of maiden, a standard reference to a woman's youth and virginity.

Marion's family home was at Blidworth, a small village in the heart of Sherwood Forest. Her father was either dead or away at the Crusades fighting in the Holy Land with King Richard, because in his absence, Marion was made a ward of court, under the protection of his brother Prince John. To mix in such exalted company would validate her position in society and confirm that Marion was probably an heiress in her own right. The problem is – which one?

The early stories have no mention of Marion, and even when she does appear they place very little emphasis on her as a person because at the time the Church suppressed women, tales ignored them, the clerics hid the fact that they even existed and playwrights gave them minor roles which were normally played by men. In the general manner of things, any woman who appeared in literature, other than one of noble birth, was slanderously declared a prostitute.

In the storyline of *Prince of Thieves*, Marion is Marion du Bois, a distant cousin of King Richard and Prince John, which might have stemmed from an earlier reference stating that Marion was the daughter of Sir Hugo de Burgh. In *Robin of Sherwood*, she is Marion of Leaford, daughter of the impoverished knight who Robin helped when the Abbot of St Mary's confiscated his land, and in Theresa Tomlinson's novel, Mary de Holt becomes Marion, a forest wife.

Many writers refer to her as Lady Marion Fitzwalter, although this seems to be a mix up with Lady Matilda Fitzwalter, daughter of Sir Richard Fitzwalter, Lord of Malaset. The *Worksop Guardian* of 16 December 1927 carried a story about the 'true identity' of Maid Marion as researched by John Martin Scudder, the London Antiquarian. He stated that Marion was the daughter of Lord Robert Fitzwalter of Essex whose family came over with William the Conqueror. They held lands around Dunmow just outside Colchester, Essex. While Marion/ Matilda was residing at Dunmow, King John constantly pestered her with his amorous advances and because she would not agree to his wicked propositions, he arranged for a servant to poison a boiled egg, which she ate. Lady Matilda Fitzwalter is buried between two stone pillars in the south side of Little Dunmow parish church, Essex.

Whoever she was, Prince John was undoubtedly enamoured with Marion because whenever he was in Nottingham area, Marion was moved, along with other members of the royal household, to wherever the royal party was. This was usually the royal hunting lodges at Bestwood, Nottingham or Clipstone.

It was while she was on her way to Clipstone that her cavalcade was ambushed by Robin and his gang, and there is every likelihood that she was carried off into the greenwood and held hostage. A huge ransom demand was probably requested for her safe return. We can only speculate about this because, after all, that's what outlaws did. What we do know is that she was eventually returned to her ward, but in the meantime had lost her heart to a wild and wilful outlaw.

In her position Marion was supposed to marry into nobility, so when she fell in love with Robin Hood this should have been a perfect match. However, it was considered highly unsatisfactory and nothing more than a romantic notion because in the social circles that she moved in, Robin Hood was an outlaw and an outcast.

With so much opposition to her choice, she decided to defy convention, escape her tight confines and make herself an outcast, but once she had made that decision there was no turning back. She was forced to denounce her old life, happy to live in the forest amongst the outlaws in order to be with the man she loved. She obviously adapted well to her new circumstances, and

Above left: Life-sized statues of Robin and Marion by Neale Andrews ARBS, at Edwinstowe.

Above right: Robin and Marion with dog from Pierce Egan's *Robin Hood and Little John,* 1840.

although Friar Tuck might have performed some sort of marriage rites under the greenwood tree, we are told 'she lives a spotless maiden life, and shall, till Robin's outlaw life has ended. Then he may lawfully take her to wife, which, if King Richard returned, will not be long.'

So they waited until after Robin's pardon for a true wedding at Edwinstowe Church. This should have been a grand celebration, a week of festivities, a wedding that all and sundry wanted to attend. The minstrels and balladeers should have been in their element, because everybody loves a wedding, so why didn't the story tellers make a big issue of this one? Okay, Marion was probably still ostracised by her family and friends, which would account for why they were not wed at her village church at Blidworth, yet surely this can't be the sole reason for such a non-event? Robin had gained his pardon: he was marrying the woman he loved and who loved him, King Richard was on the guest list, so why, when this had the potential of being a wonderfully romantic saga, was it a disappointing anticlimax?

It seems to reflect the unfortunate fact that being a woman, Marion is only given a minor part and her relationship with Robin sadly doesn't come over very strong. There are certain people who would remind me that there is a ballad called *Robin Hood and Maid Marion*, but don't get excited. It's never been in any of the major publications and a brief description of it says 'a famous battle between Robin Hood and Maid Marion; declaring their love, life and liberty', and that's about as romantic as it gets.

Briefly, Robin meets Marion while they are both in disguise and, failing to recognise each other, they fight for hours until he calls a truce. It is only then that they both realise who the other is, and if you believe that … This particular story ends with much feasting and dancing: they then retire to Robin Hood's bower where they spend the night together. There is no wedding ceremony, which is quite at odds with the image of the gentle, chaste Marion who features in other ballads.

Above left: Robin teaches Marion how to shoot from Pierce Egan's *Robin Hood and Little John,* 1840.

Above right: Festivities in Sherwood Forest, taken from a woodcut by Gilbert.

Little John

It is highly likely that the name John Little was reversed for comic effect because Little John was a giant of a man. Some stories say that he was a nail maker by trade and it has also been suggested that his real name was John Naylor or Nailor, an occupation name. His cottage, long since gone, was on Peafield Lane, the A6075 between Mansfield Woodhouse and Edwinstowe, which was the site of an old Roman road. Many of the ballads have Little John finding his way effortlessly through the forest implying that, as a local man, he is more familiar with the terrain than most. One tale has his mother, an ancient scold, acting as cook to the foresters, so she'd need to be in the vicinity to nip over to the camp on a regular basis.

Robin and Little John met when they both refused to give way while crossing a log which acted as a bridge over a stream. A fight with quarter-staffs ensued and Robin finished up in the water, but he then invited Little John to join his outlaw band and John became Robin's right-hand man. Turn by the Little John Inn on the B6020 to locate the footpath to Fountaindale where, on a bridge over a stream now culverted or dried up, they fought for supremacy.

A belief that is widely held is that Little John retired to Hathersage in the Derbyshire Peak District where he died. A ballad called 'Little John's End' was written by William Haines and published in Volume Two of the Reliquary. But why did he go to a remote place like Hathersage?

Above left: Little John knew how to impress the girls. (H. Pyle)

Above right: The Little John Inn sign.

Right: Little John and Robin fight for right of way on the bridge in this statue at the Sherwood Forest Visitor's Centre, Edwinstowe.

Little John's cottage at
Hathersage, *c.* 1847.

The Peak district in those days was a wild, isolated place and villagers kept themselves to themselves. A stranger in their midst would have been looked upon with deep suspicion. Perhaps he never forgave himself for letting his master die without realising that treachery was afoot, and went off to live like a hermit as penance or to avoid the wrath of the other members of Robin Hood's band? Whatever the reason, when he reached Hathersage he was ill and exhausted; he died and was buried. The cottage where he died, said to be east of the churchyard, has now been demolished, but a sketch survives.

Much the Miller's son

One of Robin's loyal supporters, but could someone's bad handwriting have landed Nick Miller with a name like Much? Did someone misspell or misread Nick? He's also called Midge in the tale of Allen a Dale's wedding: 'Then stepped forth brave Little John and Midge the Miller's son'. An alternative idea is that Much was derived from the Old English Muchel, which had various spellings and meant 'great'.

Will Scarlet

Will's name appeared in many forms – Scathelocke, Scathlock and Scarlok all being a reference to his red hair; 'scathe' means to burn, 'locke' means hair. His true name was Will Gamwell, and Will and Robin were related. They could have been cousins: Robin's mother Joan in *Robin Hood's Birth, Breeding, Valour and Marriage* is said to be the sister of George Gamwell of Great Gamwell Hall, Nottinghamshire. Gamston in Nottinghamshire was originally Gamelstune and land was held by Gamell at the time of the Conquest. By Robin's time it could have become Gamwell, and one married into the family.

It's also stated that Will Gamwell was the son of Robin's sister living in Mansfield, making them nephew and uncle: 'In Maxfield was I born and bred, my name is young Gamwell, and

I am his (Robin's) own sister's son,' said Will in *Robin Hood Newly Revived* (1641-74). In *Robin Hood and the Stranger*, Will's father is referred to as a noble lord and Maxfield Earl, but as no records survive this can't be confirmed. There is an old story told in Mansfield of how an ancient dwelling in the town was being demolished and a secret room was found containing a cap and clothing of Lincoln green. It didn't take long for these articles to become associated with Will Scarlet.

A more lasting monument to Will is in the churchyard at Blidworth.

Allen a Dale

Although Allen a Dale doesn't get into the action or play a major part in the ballads, as a singer and story teller he is probably the one who chronicled the adventures and put them to music. There is just one story where Allen is the star. It's called *Robin Hood and Allen a Dale* and tells how Allen married his sweetheart Ellen and joined the outlaw gang. In this ballad, we first meet Allen as a carefree young man clothed in fine, red scarlet. He's in a happy, untroubled mood, yet the next day as he walks back along the forest path, he is crestfallen and Robin wants to know why. He replies: 'Yesterday I should have married a maid but she is now from me tane, And chosen to be an old knight's delight whereby my poor heart is slain'.

Apparently, that day Allen's sweetheart Ellen was to marry an elderly Norman knight named Sir Stephen of Trent, a marriage arranged by her father Edward of Deirwold, a stout Saxon franklin, a substantial landowner of free, but not noble birth. Robin asks Allen how much he will pay to get his true love back. 'I have no money', the young man said, 'but five shillings and a ring. And that I have kept this seven long years to have it at my wedding.'

When Robin hears this, he feels sorry for the young man and agrees to help, so they all set off to stop the wedding. When they arrive, the bishop is ready and waiting; the wealthy old knight arrives with the beautiful young Ellen and Robin steps forward to halt proceedings:

> This is no fit match, quoth bold Robin Hood, that you do seem to make here
> For since we are come into the church, the bride shall chuse her own dear

The thankful bride chooses Allen, the old knight is sent on his way and rather than waste the occasion, Robin suggests that the wedding should still take place with Allen as the bridegroom. The officiating bishop insisted that the marriage would then not be legal as no banns had been called, so to remedy this, Robin takes the bishop's cape and mitre and gives them to Little John, who calls the banns seven times to make sure it's legal, and the young couple are married.

> And thus having ended this merry wedding the bride lookt as fresh as a Queen
> And so they returned to the merry green wood amongst the leaves so green

In exchange for saving Ellen from her arranged marriage, Allen joins Robin's group, and if you want to visit the little church where the wedding took place, go to Steetley Chapel.

Above left: Will Scarlet in this sculpture outside Nottingham Castle.

Above right: Allen a Dale plays the harp and sings in this sculpture outside Nottingham Castle.

Left: 'The bride shall chuse her own dear'. (H. Pyle)

Friar Tuck's statue outside
Nottingham Castle.

Friar Tuck

Friar could have been frere or brother, but definitely a man of the cloth who was brought into the tales in *Robin Hood and the Curtal Friar*. Tuck probably has the same meaning as 'curtal', which means 'corded'. This is a reference to the cord worn around their waists so they could hitch up or tuck their habits to make them more serviceable.

New recruits had to serve one year before they were allowed to become monks, at which point they were given their cord and scaplet, and had their hair cut in that strange tonsured shape. And just out of interest – what did a friar wear under his habit? Nothing while in the confines of the monastery, but if he went outside the gates, he wore a pair of pants. When he returned, he took these off and put them back in a communal cupboard ready for the next person to wear.

Friar Tuck had a close association with Lenton priory in Nottinghamshire but in the ballad *Robin Hood and the Curtal Friar*, he is living like a hermit at Fountaindale. The meeting of Friar Tuck and Robin Hood is perhaps one of the best-known tales. Each in turn carries the other across the stream, purportedly the one that once ran through Fountain Dale, then Robin is tossed into the water. In the end, all is forgiven and Tuck becomes one of the outlaw gang.

A merry Friar Tuck. (H. Pyle)

Robin is carried over the river by Friar Tuck. (H. Pyle)

Sir Richard of Lee

A Lytell Geste of Robyn Hode is generally accepted as being the first printed story of Robin's adventures and it features Sir Richard of Lee, a knight who is indebted to the Abbot of St Mary's, York, to the sum of £400. These monks were notorious moneylenders. In fact, it was a regular practice, and the monasteries acquired land and tenements in payment of loans when the people could not repay their debts.

This particular debt was caused by Sir Richard's son, who killed a Lancashire knight and his esquire, and the abbot is calling in the debt. Sir Richard is unable to pay, but after his encounter with Robin, who gives him the £400, Sir Richard sets off to face the abbot. Initially Sir Richard pretends he hasn't got the money and calls upon the good nature of the abbot, but he is corrupt, greedy and unprincipled and refuses to accept anything less than Sir Richard's estates. Fortunately, Sir Richard is able to pay off the debt, and later, not forgetting his obligation to Robin and his men, when the outlaws flee from the Sheriff's men, they take refuge at the knight's castle, described as double-ditched and walled and on the edge of Sherwood Forest. This description would perfectly fit the motte-and-bailey castle that stood at Annesley, eight miles north of Nottingham, and as there was every likelihood that the 'ley' in the name could have been spelt 'lea' or lee', which would suggest that this was the home of Sir Richard of Lee.

The High Sheriff of Nottinghamshire and Derbyshire

After the Norman Conquest, the kingdom was divided into counties and the largest town in the district, from which the county usually took its name, was the administrative centre. Thus Nottingham became the centre where the High Sheriff of Nottinghamshire and Derbyshire, the royal ambassador and, in principle, the highest law in the county lived. The Sheriff had a contingent of troops and the use of Nottingham Castle, but would have lived at the Red Lodge, at the end of what is now Angel Row. His job was to administer the law, yet he was hampered by two key issues: the collection of the King's taxes and ensuring that these taxes were transported safely and arrived at their destination intact.

If he wasn't portrayed as such an unpleasant, officious man who was constantly feathering his own nest, one could almost feel sorry for the Sheriff, because in the dense forests of Nottinghamshire many men lived outside the law. Their only means of support was Greenwood banditry, so it was an ongoing struggle for the Sheriff to invent schemes to try to outwit the outlaws and transport the taxes safely, an almost impossible task when the armed escorts could be ambushed or shot by camouflaged bowmen at every stage of the way.

There is no doubt that the Sheriff and Robin were arch-enemies, and Robin never seemed to pass up an opportunity to enrage the man. He sneaked in and out of Nottingham on a regular basis on the pretence of praying (*Robin Hood and The Monk*), entering competitions (*Robin Hood and the Silver Arrow*) and selling meat (*Robin Hood and the Butcher*) and pots (*Robin Hood and the Potter*). In this latter ballad, Robin encounters a potter at Wentbridge, takes on his guise and walks all the way to Nottingham to sell his wares. Counting the return journey, this would be a hundred-mile round trek: why did he do that when there were plenty of markets nearby? On reaching Nottingham, Robin sent some of the finest pots to the Sheriff's wife, who promptly invited him to dinner. When he left, he thanked her for her kindness and gave her a gold ring. Wasn't that a rather generous and questionable gift from a lowly potter she'd never met before – and that's as well as the pots? Yet there's more. Robin, still disguised as the potter, takes the

Sir Richard of Lee pleads with the greedy Abbot of St Mary's. (H. Pyle)

Sheriff into Sherwood Forest to meet Robin Hood, and surprise, surprise, the Sheriff and his men are soon overpowered by the outlaws. They are stripped and robbed and the Sheriff sent back to his loving wife with a white pony as a gift from Robin Hood.

Why would a man be so generous if he was not interested in the woman? Would it not be the ultimate success for Robin and humiliation for the Sheriff if Robin was having an affair with his wife? It's not the stuff of early ballads but in her position, she would have been a valuable accomplice for Robin Hood.

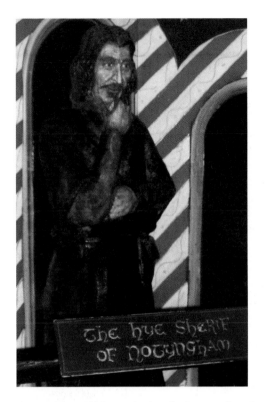

Above left: The High Sheriff of Nottinghamshire and Derbyshire in a display at the Sherwood Forest Visitor's Centre, Edwinstowe.

Above right: Robin, disguised as a butcher, sells his meat cheaply in Nottingham, but was this to impress the sheriff's wife? (H. Pyle)

In Search of Robin Hood

The naming of geographical formations, wells, boundary stones, buildings and sites traditionally associated with a famous legendary figure is nothing new, but Robin Hood and his merrie men must have far more than their fair share. I was prepared to find a good supply in Nottinghamshire, some in Yorkshire, a few in Derbyshire – but I hadn't reckoned on them spreading into the border regions of Scotland and reaching down to Surrey. Here in one small area of the Royal Borough of Kingston-on-Thames is Robin Hood's Roundabout, a traffic island just outside Robin Hood's Gate, one of the six vehicular entrances to Richmond Park on the A3, also known as Robin Hood's Way.

I was soon to find that this was not an exception. There are sites named after Robin Hood all over England and more than a scattering abroad. To list them all would be a near impossible task, yet one worthy of note (and possibly the furthest afield) is the Robin Hood Orphanage in Chitwan, Nepal, a project instigated by ex-Corporal Owen Blackwell of the Worcestershire and Sherwood Foresters Regiment. Because there must be thousands of named sites, our gazetteer is restricted to those in Robin Hood Country – Nottinghamshire, Derbyshire, Yorkshire and

Staffordshire – because this is where we also found places mentioned in the tales, ancient sites, interesting statues of the outlaws, aged artefacts, and stories of the ghosts that haunt Robin Hood Country. Each location has been numbered and for ease of following the trail, it has been divided into six areas – North Nottinghamshire, South Nottinghamshire, Nottingham, Staffordshire, Derbyshire and Yorkshire.

Above: Hunting in Sherwood Forest.

Right: Robin Hood's Gate in Richmond Park, Surrey, just off Robin Hood's Way, and Robin Hood's Roundabout.

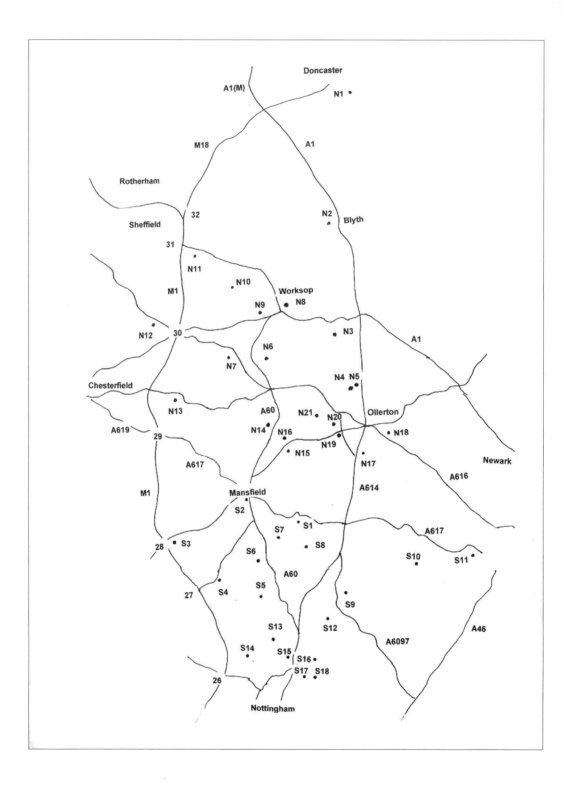

From North to Middle Nottinghamshire

Map of the area showing key sites

Key to the map:

N1	Robin Hood Airport
N2	Blyth
N3	Clumber Park
N4	Thoresby Hall
N5	Thoresby Stable Gallery
N6	Welbeck Abbey
N7	Robin Hood Cave at Creswell Crags
N8	Worksop
N9	Steetley Chapel
N10	Thorpe Salvin
N11	Todwick
N12	Renishaw Hall
N13	Bolsover Castle
N14	Warsop
N15	King John's Palace, Kings Clipstone
N16	Archway House, Clipstone
N17	Rufford Abbey
N18	Wellow
N19	Edwinstowe
N20	Sherwood Country Park and Visitor's Centre
N21	Sacred Trees and Mystical Sherwood Forest

NORTH NOTTINGHAMSHIRE

N1 ROBIN HOOD AIRPORT

Just inside the Yorkshire border, yet less than a mile west and north of Nottinghamshire, is Robin Hood Airport. It opened officially on 28 April 2005, when the first flight destined for Palma Majorca, departed at 9.15 a.m. Many people are mystified as to why Yorkshire's new international airport, six miles west of Doncaster on the site of the former RAF Finningly base in South Yorkshire, should have been given this name, but according to the airport authorities, the name is to provide an identity, raise attention and create a marketing opportunity. It's also interesting that until Government Administrative Boundary changes were made in 1974, Finningly was located in Nottinghamshire, so perhaps it's a sharing thing. Leave the airport and take the A614 to…

N2 BLYTH

In Robin Hood's time, Blyth was on the northern fringe of Sherwood Forest. It lay on the King's Great Highway, the ancient trackway between London and York, and on the route of Stone Street or the Great Way of Blyth as it was sometimes called. There was an important Benedictine monastery at Blyth built in 1088 by the Norman knight Roger de Busli. Most monastic establishments acted rather like our motorway service stations and hotel chains, and travellers were encouraged to break their journeys there. Eventually, as more and more pilgrims began travelling along the roads, the monasteries couldn't cope and inns were opened to provide food and overnight shelter.

It's therefore rather fitting that we should begin our journey at Blyth, because the earliest written story, *The Lytell Geste of Robin Hood*, opens with Robin suggesting that Little John and Will Scathelocke find a paying guest to dine with them. When they encounter an impoverished knight and offer the invitation, the knight says: 'My purpose was to have dined today at Blyth or Doncaster'. Instead he dines in the Greenwood with Robin and his men, tells them his sad tale and gains their help and friendship. His name was Sir Richard of Lee.

In the same ballad, monks travelling from York to London were stopped in a similar way and invited to dine, a privilege for which they were made to pay dearly. As the monk said: 'Me rue I came so near, for better cheap I might have dined in Blyth or Doncaster.'

N3 CLUMBER PARK

Take the A1, then the A614. Just south of Worksop is one of the finest parklands in the county, the creation of the first Duke of Newcastle who, in 1697, enclosed 3,000 acres of Sherwood Forest. It now boasts 120 different types of trees and a magnificent serpentine lake, yet the house, built by the second Duke of Newcastle in the 1760s, was demolished in 1938 and the park is now owned by The National Trust.

It was the second duke who is credited with developing the Clumber Spaniel, the heavyweight of the spaniel world, the progenitors of which are the Alpine Spaniel, the St Bernard and the Basset Hound. This aristocratic gundog is a veritable bulldozer of a dog amongst other sylph-like gun dogs. Even in its heyday as a working dog, the Clumber Spaniel was not built for speed, but neither were the mature sportsmen who, like the duke himself, were slowed down by years of good living.

The time-slip cottage and ghosts of Clumber Park

As the birthplace of the Clumber Spaniel, it would be nice to image that at least one or two of these great dogs return in spirit to romp through the long grass between the trees, but most reports

Thoresby Hall, built
on what was originally
Sherwood Forest land.

of ghostly activity in Clumber Park seem centred around the serpentine lake. Here a ghostly lady wearing a long coat or cloak of grey or pale brown is seen. She lingers on the balustraded bridge looking down into the water in a pensive mood, and although numerous people have caught a glimpse of this ethereal creature, she disappears rapidly if anyone gets too near.

John Fletcher, writer, local historian and expert on the Dukeries told me a most interesting tale about a man who approached him with the following story. The man, who visits Clumber Park regularly for recreational purposes, one day noticed a cottage deep in the woods. He couldn't remember seeing it before, but it had all the signs of habitation including children playing in the garden, so at the time he didn't think anything was amiss. Walking in the same area some time later, he couldn't find the cottage and this perplexed him so much that he returned time and time again to make a more thorough search. Having no success, he asked John's advice and John was able to tell him that there was no cottage and according to his early maps, there had never been any form of habitation in that area.

What the man had undoubtedly experienced is what is termed a time slip, a past scenario in a present day setting, so now we are left with the tantalising question; could a cottage have been there before the time of accurate maps or records? In Robin Hood's day, there might have been not only one cottage on this site, but a well-established Saxon village. Unfortunately, outside the defensive walls of a town, such unprotected places could provide no fortification against marauders and were the constant victims of attack and rapine. Though the buildings would not have been made of any lasting material, an archaeological dig might one day settle the matter: unfortunately, time slips can't be used as indisputable evidence that a small medieval community could have been here in Robin Hood's time!

N4 THORESBY HALL

Thoresby is a Danish Viking name, but the first recorded owner, Robert de Pierrepont, came to England with William the Conqueror, who gave him this piece of Sherwood Forest. His descendent was created a baron – the Earl of Kingston – by Charles I, and the 4th earl built the first recorded mansion here in 1683. This burnt down in 1745; a second hall was built in 1749, but was demolished, then the third and present Thoresby Hall was designed by Anthony Salvin in the Manorial style and built between 1864-1875.

The centrepiece of the library at Thoresby Hall is the continued chimneypiece carved from Sherwood oak, depicting a scene from the forest and statue supports of Robin Hood and Little John.

The 5th and last earl died in 1955 leaving a widow and an only daughter, Lady Rozelle Raynes, and in the spring of 1957, Thoresby Hall opened its doors to the general public for the first time. Following the death of the widowed 6th countess at the age of ninety-four in 1984, Thoresby was offered for sale, but two purchasers went bankrupt and the hall stood empty for ten years. In 1990, it was declined by The National Trust and in 1998 was put on the English Heritage at-risk register. Part of the roof had been removed and, being open to the elements, rain had ruined the ornate plaster ceilings, fungi the size of footballs grew along the cornices and fragments of once-beautiful silk wallpaper hung off the walls. Vandals moved in, smashing and stealing, and it was such an empty, echoing shell that it was chosen as the perfect setting for the creepy 'Satis House' in the BBC's 1998 production of *Great Expectations* with Charlotte Rampling as Miss Haversham. What is now the small bar was made into Miss Haversham's room; damp patches, cracked plaster and swatches of paper clinging to the walls were all part of the original fabric.

Then in 1998, this sad, neglected building was purchased by the Warner Holiday Group. With a budget of £20 million and working within the tight guidelines of a Grade I listed building, Warners have restored Thoresby Hall to its former glory and turned it into a luxury hotel and spa. New buildings now cater for the functional needs while the dignified old building with its impressive grand hall and superb reception rooms has been beautifully renovated to create a period ambience that would not have been out of place one hundred years ago when still a family home. Marble chimney pieces and rococo panelling, elaborate, highly decorated ceilings and cornices have been painstakingly restored to produce a sense of grandeur that is usually only found in the sterile surroundings of our heritage-owned country houses.

The great hall, dominated by an elaborate stone fireplace embellished with the Pierrepont coat-of-arms, really lives up to its name: 64ft long, 31ft wide and 50ft in height, it rises through three storeys to an open hammer beam roof. In the blue room, which takes its name from the silk damask which covered the walls, guests dine in the luxury setting of the ex-dining room to the nobility. The library, still well furnished with books, occupies the centre of the south front suite, which looks out over the south terrace and the gardens created during the landscape movement of the eighteenth and nineteenth centuries. It's possible to stroll along the gravel walkways between manicured lawns and colourful flower beds, play croquet, or sit in one of the two 1860 stone gazebos while contemplating the amazing view.

Above, left and right: The finely carved statues of the two outlaw friends, Robin Hood and Little John, in more mature years.

But the reason for my visit was to check out a totally unique, continued chimneypiece carved from local Sherwood oak. After hearing all the tales of doom and destruction, I expected to be told it had been pulled out and sold or smashed to pieces, but no, I was delighted to find the double- storey surround has not only survived, but is still the focal point of the library. The only signs of damage seem to have been caused by the heat of an open fire.

To say the piece is huge is no understatement. It's actually 14ft high by 10ft wide. On either side of the fireplace opening are finely wrought statues of Robin Hood and Little John standing around 4ft high. They are superbly crafted, and what is quite charming about this pair is that they are looking old and tired. Little John stands tall and straight although his hands rest on his staff, while Robin leans heavily on one knee and looks worn out.

The panel above the mantel shelf, with its deep, distinct patina, is a scene of Sherwood Forest carved in low relief: there's the Major Oak, a herd of deer and a foreground of beautifully rendered fern, and what makes this whole piece even more special is the fact that it was produced from indigenous oak and took local, Mansfield craftsmen over three years to carve. As with all my enquiries I asked the helpful staff if Thoresby Hall is haunted: the question seemed to cause some confusion, yet no tales of any significance, so I wonder who was with me at Thoresby Hall? I ask this in all seriousness because when I got the photographs of the fireplace printed, there is a definite orb over on the right on the edge of the carved scene.

Above: This photograph of the panel above the mantelshelf definitely shows an orb over on the right and possibly another on a line in the centre, so what ghostly entity was with me at Thoresby Hall?

Left: Robin Hood drawing his bow, as depicted by Tussaud-Birt.

N5   THE STABLE GALLERY AT THORESBY

Next to Thoresby Hall, with convenient access via the car park for hotel guests, the old stables have been beautifully converted into craft shops. In keeping with its location in Sherwood Forest, in the centre of the courtyard is a stone statue of a young Robin Hood in his customary pose drawing his bow. This statue was made in 1948 by Tussaud-Birt, a grandson of Madame Tussaud of waxwork fame.

N6   WELBECK ABBEY

Apart from a few minor roads and Robin Hood's Way, the registered footpaths and bridleways that form a continuous themed route round Nottinghamshire, there is no public access to Welbeck. As an abbey, it was founded in 1153 by the white canons of the Premonstratensian Order from Lincolnshire under Thomas de Cuckney. They cleared and cultivated the land at Welbeck, an area that would have been familiar to Robin and his men.

After the Dissolution of the monasteries, the estate came into the possession of the Dukes of Portland, who transformed it into their family seat. In the 1950s, much of Welbeck Abbey was leased to the Army to become Welbeck Military College, but in 2006 the army moved out placing Welbeck back in family ownership. Welbeck Abbey is strictly private but on the site of the nineteenth-century gasworks that supplied the Welbeck estate is The Harley Gallery. Built in 1994, this venue offers an award-winning gallery that features a diverse exhibition programme, a craft shop and café, plus the neighbouring Dukeries Garden Centre.

N7   ROBIN HOOD'S CAVE AT CRESWELL CRAGS

This magnificent limestone valley lies on the Nottinghamshire/Derbyshire border. It is one of the oldest known inhabited places in Britain and in the caves on each side of the valley have been found remains of many prehistoric animals and the earliest known remains of modern man in Britain from 13,000 years ago.

The caves were frequented by Robin Hood, and would have made a perfect hideout for the outlaw gang, so it is not surprising that one of the caves now bears his name. In one of the Robin Hood ballads, Robin and his men trick Prince John into going to the crags to supposedly locate the outlaws, although as usual it is a hoax. While Prince John and his men are searching the crags, Robin releases the prisoners held in the dungeons at his palace at Clipstone.

N8 WORKSOP

Worksop has always been a tourist centre and back in Robin Hood's day, people would have come to Worksop for medicinal purposes. The Augustinian canons who resided at the priory here were famous for their production of liquorice, a plant native to southern Europe and Asia, brought to Britain from the Middle East at the time of the Crusades.

Liquorice is the root of a shrub related to the pea family and was cultivated in many monastery gardens for its medicinal purposes. It has been used as ear drops and to flavour foul-tasting medicines; to treat peptic ulcers, arthritis, allergies, eczema, herpes, shingles, mouth ulcers, headaches, clear toxins out of the liver, and as a hangover cure. In the medieval period it would have been considered a wonder drug. The plant obviously thrived at Worksop because of the high concentration of clay in the soil but by 1825, the last garden growing this plant had been dug up. Now the only connection is 'The Liquorice Garden' a Wetherspoon's pub in the centre of the town where you can take light refreshment – or perhaps a Guinness or sambuca, both drinks flavoured with liquorice.

The Norman priory building, some of which is still standing, was begun in 1145 and erected on behalf of the De Lovetot family, who were lords of the manor. A piece in one of the earliest editions of the *Worksop Guardian*, dated 3 July 1896, asked the question, 'did Robin Hood ever enter Worksop Priory?' They concluded that he may have entered to pay his respects to the Augustinian canons who resided there, but it's highly unlikely that the monk-hating Robin would ever have done so by invitation – but may have by force.

The priory church of Our Lady and St Cuthbert with its impressive twin towers is still a striking feature of Worksop, particularly when viewed from Memorial Road. When the graveyard was being reorganised recently, an ancient human skull with an arrowhead embedded in it was discovered. It is alleged to be a Sherwood Forester killed by none other than Robin Hood, but who knows? It now has its own small, glass-fronted niche near the back of the priory church.

The Priory's Ghosts

According to a report in the *Worksop Guardian* on 15 January 1988, there is a monk who walks the transept in the priory church on Midsummer's Eve. People have also reported hearing footsteps in that area when no one is there. A ghostly woman in blue is regularly reported round the Lady Chapel. A regular visitor said that he had been walking towards the Lady Chapel when the door unlatched itself, opened, then slowly closed although there was no draught to account for this. A church flower arranger constructed a large floral display in one of the transepts, yet next morning she found it all over the floor. She was mystified because she had done similar displays many times before and always made a point of checking they were perfectly stable.

The ghostly woman in blue seems to be active both inside and out. Many people have reported seeing 'the blue lady' as she walks the path between the fourteenth-century gatehouse and the priory church. One man claims to have seen her on numerous occasions while walking past the priory late at night. His friend also confirmed that he too had felt some ghostly presence in the grounds and seen 'something' sitting in a tree. An ex-pupil of the Abbey Girls' School who had some of her lessons in the priory gatehouse recalled that she and her school friends would

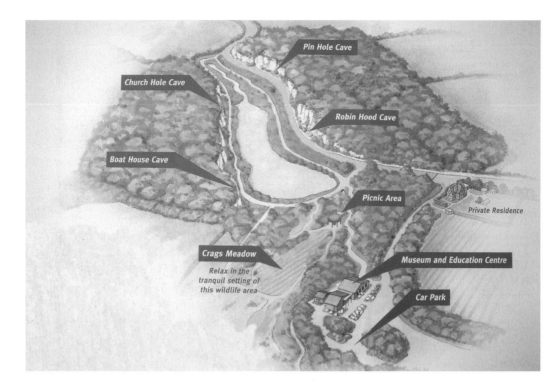

Above: An aerial sketch of Creswell Crags showing Robin Hood's Cave.

Left: The ruins of Worksop Priory where the resident monks grew liquorice, the medieval wonder drug.

talk about a blue lady who would sit on a funny shaped tree just down from the gatehouse. They all date her clothing as being from the medieval period, and all agree she sits on an oddly shaped branch, set at a right angle to the trunk of one of the trees that line the path from the church to the gatehouse. In the autumn of 2004 a chef was walking home late one night from the restaurant in Worksop where he worked when he saw what he thought was a fellow late-night worker or reveller. He didn't pay too much attention until she suddenly disappeared before his eyes.

Above: The skull found at Worksop Priory.

Right: The ghost of a medieval lady is seen inside and outside the priory church, Worksop, and an Augustinian canon is regularly seen on top of one of these two priory towers.

It is said that a tunnel leads from the priory church to the Lion Hotel, a Georgian house on Bridge Street, and there have been reports of phantom monks walking in this tunnel. For many years there were tales of another underground tunnel that linked the priory gatehouse to the site of the castle, two miles away. This also was purportedly haunted by the Black Canons of Worksop.

From tunnels to towers, the ghost of an Augustinian canon is regularly seen on top of one of the two priory towers. According to reports, he is in a state of high excitement or possibly agitation. He runs round the top of the tower then jumps up and down, and periodically peers over the walls. Many have seen this ghostly monk but why he acts in such a strange way is a mystery. Perhaps he has just discovered that liquorice can cure all known ills and is wondering how to cash in on the idea before anyone else finds out!

N9 STEETLEY CHAPEL

Head out of Worksop on the A619, and continue for about one mile, then take a minor right turn marked to Shireoaks and Thorpe. After about 300 yards take left turn and just off this junction is the most perfectly preserved little Norman church. This little gem is called Steetley Chapel yet it is not marked on maps or road signs. Lying on the borders of Nottinghamshire/ Derbyshire, this is undoubtedly one of the oldest and most attractive buildings in Sherwood Forest. It was built in around 1140 by Gley de Briton as his private chapel; traditionally Friar Tuck regularly took the outlaws here to pray. It's also said that Steetley Chapel had a false roof in which Robin and his men hid when necessary.

This tiny chapel has a semi-circular apse at the end of the nave, a feature that was copied in many of the early Christian churches. The marvel is that this beautiful church has weathered so

Left: Did Robin and his men watch from this window while hiding at Steetley Chapel?

Opposite: The Norman chapel at Steetley where the outlaws hid and Allen a Dale was purportedly married.

many storms. It stood deserted and derelict for over 200 years, was used as a shed for lumber, yet was skilfully restored in 1882 and reconsecrated. It is now part of the parish of Whitwell and a service is held here every Sunday at 3.15 p.m.

Although it seems quite out of proportion for such a small building, 56ft in length by 16ft wide, enter by the magnificent south doorway with its four round arches. The outer arch, with zigzag mouldings, rests on columns carved with signs of the zodiac, although these are now indecipherable as they've been damaged by exposure. A massive chancel arch has a scene of Saint George slaying the dragon, and a second arch divides the chancel from the apse, the vault of which is supported by ribs resting on pillars carved with beak-heads.

In the tale of Robin Hood and Allen a Dale, Robin intervenes to prevent Allen's sweetheart Ellen marrying an elderly Norman knight named Sir Stephen of Trent, a marriage arranged by her father Edward of Deirwold, a stout Saxon franklin. Although the church is not named, it is described as 'a certain little church that belonged to a private estate', and although we can never be 100 per cent sure that this is the church, its been accepted as such for hundreds of years.

N10   THORPE SALVIN
Despite the fact that most people accept that Robin Hood was buried at Kirklees and Little John was buried in Hathersage, this area makes a rather startling claim. Allegedly, Robin is buried in the farm next to Steetley churchyard, and if you continue on this lane for a mile, in Thorpe Salvin churchyard is the last resting place of Little John.

N11   TODWICK
Head for the A57 towards the M1, junction 31, and the village of Todwick just over the border in South Yorkshire. Here an oak tree has a plaque containing this inscription – 'On this site

once stood Robin Hood's Trysting Tree, immortalised in Walter Scott's Ivanhoe'. Despite a public outcry, the original oak was felled in 1961 to make room for some bungalows, and was ultimately replaced by a sapling of the Major Oak planted on the 18 May 1974 by Gerald F. Young, Lord Lieutenant of Yorkshire. By the same tradition, an oak tree standing within a few yards of this was known as Robin Hood's Larder.

N12   RENISHAW HALL

Take the M1 down to junction 30 then the A6135 to Eckington. Within a mile, you will arrive at Renishaw Hall. The gardens, open from the end of March to October, are a delight, the old stable block houses the Gallery Café and three galleries, plus the Sitwell museum, but the hall is still very much a family home and private. It is however occasionally possible to have a guided tour of the ground floor rooms, and if you are fortunate enough to, the highlight of the visit for any Robin Hood aficionado is seeing what is said to be Robin Hood's longbow. Granted, relics are notoriously prone to falsification, but this is considered the real thing. The bow was moved from Kirklees Hall in the late 1600s and according to a booklet of 1700 it resided for a time at Fountains Abbey. From there it was moved to Barlborough Hall, the seat of the de Rode family on the Derbyshire/Nottinghamshire border, hardly a mile away from Renishaw Hall. According to Sir Reresby Sitwell of Renishaw Hall, his uncle Sir Osbert Sitwell spoke of seeing the bow hanging on the wall of the front hall at Barlborough Hall when he was a boy. The property had then passed from the de Rode to the Locker-Lampson family, the last of whom was Mrs Henry Rimington Wilson who in 1939 sold up. The hall was bought by the Jesuits and made into a prep school for Mount St Mary's Public School at Spinkhill, and Sir Osbert bought much of the park and farm property and cottages of the estate.

Sir Reresby Sitwell with
Robin Hood's bow.

Bolsover Castle.

Robin Hood's bow was acquired by a Mr Fox, principle of the technical college at Worksop. Finally, in November 1949, when the bow and accompanying letter came under the auctioneers hammer, it was sold to Sir Osbert for £27. Two-and-a-half years later, on 8 August 1952, the *Worksop Guardian* ran the following story:

> Talk of archery calls to mind the sale in November 1949 at Worksop of a bow reputed to have belonged to Robin Hood. After brisk bidding, the relic was knocked down under the auctioneer's hammer to Sir Osbert Sitwell, the author, for £27. There was authentification for the bow written in mid-seventeenth century handwriting. The document describes how Robin Hood sought refuge at Kirklees Priory, now Kirklees Hall where one of his relatives was lady abbess. He was very ill and in an effort to cure him, he was bled to death. The Abbess took possession of the bow. Mr H.C. Hall of Ruddington who was at the same auction as Sir Osbert said that he had been determined to get the bow for Nottingham. He kept on bidding up to £26, but seeing that Sir Osbert was determined to get it at any price, he decided to give up. Later Mr Hall received a promise from Sir Osbert that if he ever did decide to part with it, he would let him know. So there is still a chance that the bow may find a way to the Museum at Nottingham Castle. The bow is to be on show at Worksop in the near future.

Sir Reresby Sitwell can expand upon this. He told me that after the sale, a porter handed the bow to Sir Osbert: it slipped from his grip, fell to the floor and smashed to smithereens. It cost Sir Osbert another £19 to get it repaired.

The bow, of spliced or laminated yew, is now a treasured possession and hangs above the curious triple chimneypiece in the smoke room; with the bow is the framed letter giving its known history:

> Robin Hood's Bow was given to Mr Bartlett by the family at Kirklees Hall in Yorkshire, which was formerly a nunnery, a relation of his being the Lady Abbess and to which Robin flew for safety, and tradition says that he was taken ill there and ordered to be bled. His relation procured a hole to be cut in the bottom of the porringer by which he bled to death. He was buried in the park where his gravestone is still to be seen. His bow was given to Mr Bartlett upward of forty years ago and has been in the house beyond memory of man and was always considered Robin's.

(The mysterious Mr Bartlett seems to have been related to both the lady abbess at Kirklees Priory and to the de Rodes family of Barlborough Hall.) Leave Renishaw Hall and retrace your steps back towards the MI, then take the A616 to Clowne, then the B6147 (A632) to Bolsover.

N13   BOLSOVER CASTLE
Before the Norman conquest, Bolsover was in the Saxon kingdom of Mercia; then, in 1066, William the Conqueror granted the manor and 161 others to his illegitimate son William Peveril, who was also put in charge of the Royal Forest of Sherwood. The first written mention of Sherwood Forest in 1154 states: 'William Peverill in the first year of Henry I answers to the Pleas of the Forest.' This succession of Peverils, who all seem to have had the name William, would have had the whole profit and command of Sherwood Forest; then the Peverils went out of favour when they backed the wrong side against the new King Henry II in 1152. After this, the Royal Forest of Sherwood devolved to the Crown and was managed by the High Sheriff of Nottingham and Derbyshire. This would account for why there was hostility

between Robin Hood and the Sheriff, yet no tales of friction between Robin Hood and the Peverils.

By the twelfth century, William Peveril had built a rudimentary castle at Bolsover as part of the fortification of the rocky ridge, and Peveril Castle in the Peak District, which still gives us the best clues as to what a medieval castle would have looked like. William Peveril is also credited with building the first Nottingham Castle in stone, but the Peverils lost their castles, which from then on were held by the King and run by a constable appointed by him. In 1173, it is recorded that £135 was spent on knights and their servants at Bolsover, Peveril and Nottingham Castles. Amongst other duties, these knights would have been employed to transport the King's taxes and capture Robin Hood.

Bolsover Castle changed hands many times until Charles Cavendish acquired it in 1608. By this time, castles were built to impress rather than defend, and having inherited a love of building from his mother, the indomitable Bess of Hardwick, by 1613 he had laid the foundations for the Bolsover castle we see today. It was Charles' son Sir William Cavendish who continued the build with his designer Robert Smythson, producing a strange mix of old and new ideas. During this time Sir William purchased Nottingham Castle, a broken-down, burnt-out shell, and proceeded to build the Palladian-style structure we see there today. But just imagine what would have happened if things had been reversed: Bolsover Castle might have dominated the skyline of Nottingham, and Nottingham's Palladian-style castle been sited on the high Derbyshire ridge at Bolsover.

The ghosts of Bolsover Castle

Evidence of ghostly activity at Bolsover dates back to medieval times. In fact, Bolsover's ghosts are so numerous, it's difficult to know how many to include here, so I'll just give a brief mention of the most reported ones.

Visitors regularly experience being pushed or ushered along by unseen forces. The sound of galloping horses has been heard coming up the south drive and at one re-enactment, the costumed participants were joined by extra figures. People who live on the hill below the castle often see strange, unaccountable lights flickering around the ruined Terrace Range, and in the garden of the Little Castle, where the core of the wall is Norman, knights have been seen walking around the top.

A lady in grey walks through the garden, a little boy takes the hand of visiting children, and the sound of horses and electrical tripping is frequent in the Riding House. In the Little Keep, visitors have reported hearing footsteps, objects moving, and seeing hazy figures and blue mists. Spectral scents reported include smoke from the kitchen fire, food cooking, ladies' perfume, pipe smoke and dogs. In Sir William's favourite room, people have experienced the scent of pipe smoke and perfume, but these don't last long because a Victorian housekeeper still appears to be doing her job and keeping an eye on things.

N14 WARSOP

Leave Bolsover on the A632 and branch off to Warsop which, despite its variation in spelling over the centuries, really says it all. Translated, 'op' means valley, and *wearg* is Old English for outlaw, so now you really are in the valley of the outlaw. This is the area where Robin Hood and his men sought sanctuary. The saying 'they leave their doors open in Warsop' refers not to the crime-free, good old days, but to the time when every house in the village provided a bolt-hole for fugitives from the law.

The Ghost in the Meadow

Last century, miners on their early shift would walk from Church Warsop to Welbeck colliery taking a short cut across what was then the Rectory Meadows, between the A60 and Eastlands Lane, an area that has since been built on. The miners often talked of a man who was in the habit of suddenly materialising out of the early morning mist. They never saw him closely or could describe his attire as anything other than sombre working clothes, but he was not a fellow miner and, rather strange for such a small community, no one knew who he was or why he should be wandering around the area so early. He moved noiselessly, never spoke and seemed deep in thought, but one collier who met the man one damp summer morning turned to watch him go and realised that although he could clearly see his own footprints in the long, dewy grass, the stranger had left no trace.

The Twelve Spectral Figures

Sookholm Chapel near Warsop has been a place of worship for over 1,000 years, and back in the 1930s a local man saw a vision that may have dated from that early age. As he told a local paper:

> I was alone, pausing to fill my pipe. In the distance, dense woods enfolded in an inky blackness, silhouetted against a blue/green sky. No sound save the occasional hooting of a brown owl and once, the shrill clamour of migrating birds passing overhead. For no reason at all, my attention became fixed upon the middle of an open space and presently the moonlight seemed to become more centralised, concentrating in a definite form. Quite distinctly now, before me stood a line of spectral figures, in concealing hoods and flowing robes. They were semi-transparent and diffused. I counted them. There were twelve. As I watched they arranged themselves one behind the other, with their hands placed high on each other's shoulders. They then moved off in a silent, wavering motion, moved across the moonlight space and vanished in the darkness.

Leave Warsop on the B6035 to Clipstone, but at the A6075 intersection, make a slight detour by turning right towards Mansfield Woodhouse. After about a mile on your right you will see a three-storey red-brick building called The Red Brick House Restaurant and Conference Centre. Previously a farm, I was told that it is haunted by a ghost they call Charlie. He walks the same path, which, since the extension, is across the front of the restaurant, and numerous people have felt him brush past.

'Has anyone ever seen him?' I asked.

'Oh yes. He's an elderly man dressed in a cape and hat and we think he's possibly a fisherman because he carries what looks like a fishing rod.'

'Could it possibly be a long bow rather than a fishing rod?' I asked. 'After all this is Robin Hood country.'

This obviously posed a question they'd never considered before, but perhaps next time when Charlie materialises they'll rename him Robin!

N15   PRINCE JOHN'S PALACE, KING'S CLIPSTONE

Marked on most maps as Old Clipstone – it is old because it's actually mentioned in the Domesday Book – about three years ago the name was changed to King's Clipstone in recognition of the scanty remains of King John's Palace, standing half forgotten in the middle of a hay field.

It was built originally as a church by King Edwin, the first Christian King of Northumbria, and dramatically extended later by Henry I into the building that King John would have known.

Left: Is this the ghost of the Victorian Housekeeper still keeping an eye on things? Well no, but the orbs are genuine.

Opposite: The remains of King John's Palace at Clipstone.

It was used as a hunting lodge by every English King that visited Sherwood to hunt the royal deer and provided stabling for over two hundred horses.

Prince John stayed there frequently and the site became known as King John's Palace. (He was made King in 1199 after the death of his brother King Richard). It was there that he entertained his royal and noble guests, and held Parliament. Those wealthy guests obviously provided rich pickings for Robin and his men, and legend has it that they ambushed a particularly wealthy cavalcade on their way to Clipstone and amongst the party was Lady Marion.

Marion had been made a ward of court under the protection of Prince John while her father was away at the Crusades with King Richard, and apparently Prince John was enamoured by this beautiful, chaste young heiress. The tales of Robin Hood may have been re-written if Robin hadn't waylaid her party and carried Marion off into the greenwood. Initially, he probably intended to claim a ransom for her return and extort a huge sum of money from her royal guardian but things turned out rather differently. After some dalliance, she was returned, but that initial meeting sealed her fate for ever. She had lost her heart to this dashing young outlaw and as the feeling was mutual: this seemed reason enough to trigger off the mutual hatred between Robin and Prince John.

There is every possibility that Marion was kept at Clipstone under house arrest, on instructions from Prince John, so Robin probably employed much ingenuity and many guises so that he could visit her there. We know that on one occasion the outlaws dressed as minstrels, entered the palace and released the prisoners in the dungeons after luring Prince John and his men away to the caves at Cresswell Crags in a fruitless search for them.

It was while on route to Clipstone that King John died in 1210. The palace was destroyed by fire in 1220, rebuilt by Henry III in 1270, and fell into disuse in the fifteenth century. Now this once magnificent royal hunting lodge is reduced to a few remnants of stone walling that, according to *Quaint Lore of Nottingham* by S. Coleman, are supposedly haunted by the ghost of an old lady in black who, for some unspecified reason, he links with a similar apparition at Rufford Abbey, despite the two sites being several miles apart.

As King John's Palace would have covered a vast area and I had conveniently parked in the car park of the Dog and Duck, two short fields away from the ruins, I asked Nick, the owner,

if he had heard of any hauntings in the area and he looked rather bemused. 'We've had strange problems ever since we moved in,' he confirmed. 'Pools of water mysteriously appear on the floor, taps turn themselves on so fully that it's necessary to turn off the mains water supply, but we never thought of it as ghostly activity.'

Other staff members told how they had seen shadowy figures, glasses breaking, electrics turning off and on, and pans in the kitchen swinging without any logical explanation. I asked if they ever heard or saw anything out of the ordinary over by the ruins of the old palace.

'You'd be amazed at the sights and sounds we experience round here, but that's quite usual after closing time,' they laughed. 'Do you ever see any strange, mysterious lights round the ruins?' I asked. 'I can't think of any specific incidents,' said Nick, 'but if we do, we just assume it's someone with a torch walking their dog or the lights of a parked car, but we'll keep our eyes open in future.'

N16   ARCHWAY HOUSE

If you have parked in the car park of the Dog and Duck, it is possible to walk to Archway House or alternatively, drive across the B6030, because straight opposite the entrance is Archway Road. There is a 'no through road' sign as a warning of its unadopted state, but if you steer round the pot holes and don't mind the muddy ford, drive for just over half a mile and you will encounter Archway House on your right.

Although Archway House does not have the antiquity to warrant its inclusion here, it is the ornamentation that is so fascinating. Built as a picturesque folly in 1842 by the Duke of Portland, it is often referred to as the Duke's Folly. In some ways it resembles the gatehouse at Worksop with buttressed walls and traceried windows on each side of the central arch.

The façade however, is decorated with carvings of forest life, and set in niches on the north side are statues of Friar Tuck, King Richard I and Allen a Dale. In niches on the south side are statues of Robin Hood in Saxon dress, Little John and Maid Marion, although some people say this lady is Clorinda, Queen of the Shepherds. This is probably because in *A New Ballad of Robin Hood: showing his birth, breeding, valour and marriage*, the marriage is to Clorinda, not Marion.

Could Clorinda have been his first love? It's highly possible because in this ballad Clorinda agreed to marry Robin after they had been to Tutbury Fair and they were married by the Parson of Doveridge, probably in the custom of the day under the Yew Tree in Doveridge churchyard. Archway House was once a school and is now a fine country residence shared by two families. It is also haunted by several presences, believed to be female servants or maids. One of the residents saw a spectral figure walk across the kitchen and through the outside door. The figure continued to walk away, but left no footsteps on the snow-covered ground.

The front-elevation niches of Archway House decorated with statues of Maid Marion, Robin Hood and Little John.

N17   RUFFORD ABBEY

Rufford Abbey dates back to 1147 when it was built on behalf of the Archbishop of Lincoln, Gilbert de Gaunt, as a Cistercian abbey. Yet the monks never seemed to be satisfied and grabbed all the land around, some of which included the royal forest of Sherwood. Records show that they had twenty one granges and farms, and in a fifteen-year period, they felled 7,000 oaks and 1,000 saplings to clear forest land for farming.

Their greed was unstoppable. They took no account of the needs of the locals who relied on the forest for their livelihood as the villages of Rufford, Cratley, Grimston, Besthorpe, Winkerfield, Westhaw and Almton disappeared under their onslaught. The people were moved out of their homes, often by force, and this exploitation understandably made the monks very unpopular. It is highly possible that Robin Hood was affected by this wholesale manipulation and abuse, but even if he wasn't directly involved, this is just the kind of injustice that he would have fought against.

As the monastic lands grew (and before any accurate maps recorded the borders of Rufford), the monks reorganised the roads so that any paths or highways that had previously run across their land were made to skirt round it.

With this kind of exploitation it's easy to see why the local peasants hated the monks almost as much as the domineering Norman barons, so the tales of Robin and his men taking from the avaricious monks were always greeted with great enthusiasm. Robbing the King's collectors and wealthy monks was considered an honourable kind of thievery if you could get away with it, and Robin seemed to be invincible.

After the Dissolution of the monasteries, the Rufford estate was granted to the Earl of Shrewsbury and over the years, the abbey has been changed and rebuilt numerous times until in the 1930s it fell into disrepair and neglect. Today only part of the once-impressive building remains intact and it now houses a restaurant, craft centre and shop. The undercroft that was the monk's dining room also serves as an information centre with an interesting exhibition; the roofless ruins are well worth a visit and the surrounding park has a very pleasant walk all round the lake.

Haunted Rufford

The abbey is now run jointly by Nottinghamshire County Council and English Heritage, who make quite a feature of the site's spectres. A little old lady in black wanders through the park, and a white lady is seen in the ruins. A figure garbed in the white woollen habit of a Cistercian monk glides around the place wringing ghostly hands and bemoaning the loss of the abbey. But what about all those discontented peasants from the twelfth century who, led by Robin Hood, might be out to seek revenge?

By far the most sinister spectre is the Black Friar. (Although the Cistercian monks wore white, for practical purposes they also wore dark brown tunics with a hooded brown woollen cloak). People who have seen him say he is truly terrifying. He will walk up to a person, his hood pulled down to hide his face, but as he gets close, he lifts his head, flicks back his hood and reveals a grinning skull. On 3 December 1901, an Edwinstowe man visiting Rufford saw the ghostly monk and collapsed in fright; he died soon after.

N18   WELLOW

In 1086 when William sent his inspectors to record the area for the Domesday Book, there was no Wellow, yet the parish was large and contained such villages and hamlets as Grimston, Besthorpe, Winkerfield, Cratley, Westhaw, Rufford and Almton. There is now no trace of any to them. Some historians say the people were killed off by plague or the dreaded disease of leprosy, which was brought into England by crusaders returning from Palestine, but it's more likely that when the Cistercian monks arrived at Rufford in 1146, they ousted the people to claim the neighbouring lands for themselves.

So what happened to the people? It's possible that they became outlaws. There were few alternatives for poor, starving Saxons who had lost their homes and livelihoods until Sir Robert Foliate, who had a castle near Grimstone on the edge of Sherwood Forest, proposed to create a completely new, fortified village to be called Wellow. It's an Anglo Saxon name: *Wehag* means enclosure by the well or spring, and within its protective surroundings grew a self-sufficient community.

Tony Molyneux-Smith, in his fascinating book *Robin Hood and the Lords of Wellow*, made the startling suggestion that Sir Robert Foliate was in fact Robin Hood, and the village of Wellow was the headquarters of the outlaw gang. From here the men, camouflaged in green, carried out their nefarious deeds, but returned on a regular basis. Here they grew crops, tended livestock, lived a normal life, married, had children and provided for their families. Tony's theory does have a logical foundation and it's not implausible, but surely a static community, however secretive and well protected, would soon have been at the mercy of the King's soldiers.

On the other hand, in the ballads and books the basic aspects of surviving in the greenwood are generally glossed over; the rigours of outdoor life are overlooked and the fact that harsh winters, freezing conditions and exposure can kill doesn't even enter into the equation. Fundamental housekeeping is not the stuff of ballads but I do wonder who looked after this army of men. There's no mention of any provisions other than the King's venison, despite constantly inviting paying guests to dine with them.

Who toiled over the camp-stove all day cooking their meals? Who fetched their water, collected and stored provisions, did the laundry etc etc? In one play I found these tasks were done by Little John's mother, who was described as 'an ancient scold', but this just reinforces the fact that the outlaws must have had the support of family and former neighbours who would supply them with their domestic needs, specialist workers and information. They would be willing to do this in return for the occasional 'tax rebate' and remuneration in the form of a hunk of venison. Many lords and gentry also gave food, shelter and money to the outlaws and were termed 'maintainers'.

Contrary to Tony's theory, a nomadic lifestyle meant freedom to move over a vast area, to strike where least expected and then melt away into the woodland to strike again somewhere else. If the soldiers got too close, the outlaws could slip into Yorkshire where the High Sheriff of Nottingham and Derbyshire had no jurisdiction, and there are reports of Robin nipping over the Yorkshire moors to Whitby for a change of air.

So, do you think Robin could have had a permanent base and if so, was it Wellow? This unique village, with its distinctive village green in the shape of an arrow head, was granted permission in 1268 to hold a market, and it now has one of only three permanent maypoles in England. Although records of this only go back to 1856, a maypole has stood on Wellow village green much longer. A new pole was erected in 1860 when the old one was sawn down by drunken revellers; another was erected in 1887 to celebrate Queen Victoria's Golden Jubilee. This was replaced in 1923 and again in 1937 when it was cut down from 60ft to 20ft. New poles were erected in 1949, 1950, 1966 and 1976 when the pole was considered unsafe and reduced to 10ft. All these had been larch poles from the Thoresby estate, but, in 1977, a three-section, 60ft, tubular steel pole was erected.

The grinning monk of Rufford Abbey.

Annually over 2,000 visitors flock to watch the traditional maypole dances like the Gypsies' Tent, Single Plait, Spider's web and Amo Amas. To celebrate the millennium, St Swithin's church, just off the village green, commissioned a superb stained-glass window, the topic being the Wellow maypole.

Even the village ghost story is linked to the maypole. *The Chronicle Advertiser* covered the story, which began with strange happenings at the Durham Ox, in November 1977. Apparently footsteps had been heard on the stairs, the licensee's six year-old daughter regularly talked to a person invisible to others then a phantom little grey lady walked straight past Mrs Renshaw, the landlady. The mystery deepened when Mrs Renshaw saw the little grey lady in a 1930s photograph hanging in the Olde Red Lion. It's a photograph of village children dancing round the maypole and in the middle of the crowd is the mystery phantom!

The Olde Red Lion also has its share of ghostly visitors including an old regular, and a boy in the cellars who fell down the well. It has been suggested that this well, situated in the vaulted cellar, could predate any building on the site and may have been the original well from which the village took its name.

The Grimston Ghost

Like most village children, those of Wellow have been weaned on tales that have been handed down for generations, and one of them is the tale of the Grimston Ghost who wanders the fields where the vanished villages once stood. But this is no ordinary ghost: this is purportedly the ghost of Robin Hood.

Tony Molyneux-Smith encountered him one Autumn evening as he gazed across the low hills in the direction of Wellow. To use his quote: '… how still it was. There was no birdsong, and curiously no traffic. Even the usual clatter of agricultural machinery was absent. It was as though time stood still and the village had been abandoned.'

Then Tony's attention was caught by a movement on the skyline about quarter of a mile away. It was a hooded figure carrying what appeared to be a long quarterstaff or pole and an unstrung

Above left: The village of Wellow with its maypole on the village green.

Above right: Could the Grimston ghost be Robin Hood?

bow or pike. As he watched, the figure stopped. 'I could see he was looking in my direction and for what seemed like an age, we regarded each other,' said Tony. 'Then he turned slowly and continued his steady progress through the fields and gradually disappeared in the growing darkness.

N19   EDWINSTOWE

Being in a prime position in the heart of Sherwood Forest, Edwinstowe has an unparalleled association with the Robin Hood Legend. The village was named after Edwin, the first Christian King of Northumbria, and 'stow', an Anglo Saxon name meaning 'holy place'. Edwin died at Hatfield in 633AD in a battle between the pagans of Mercia and the Christians of Northumberland. His headless body was brought to this spot and buried in a clearing in the forest now under St Mary's church. This tranquil church was purportedly where Robin and Marion married under the greenwood tree.

Although small, the village has a number of interesting shops and numerous pubs. The Maid Marion is the most aptly named, the Black Swan is the oldest, and the Edwinstowe's Dukeries hotel has a visual link with the legend. Now a Ma Hubbard's, this mock-Elizabethan structure was built in 1897 to accommodate tourists arriving by the newly built railway. The original building was rebuilt after a fire in 1929 and has undergone much improvement since, yet the supports of the canopied entrance porch remain the same. These are rather enchanting wooden carvings grouped in pairs; Robin and Marion, Little John and possibly Allen a Dale, with Friar Tuck looking down from the centre.

Outside the library on the main street of Edwinstowe is a life-size bronze statue of Robin and Marion by Neale Andrews ARBS. It was unveiled on 23 July 1998 by Councillor Chris Winterton of Nottingham County Council. It is simple, timeless and absolutely charming. She wears flowers in her hair and holds a bunch of flowers in her left hand. He holds his cap in his hand, has a dagger by his side but his bow, slung round his left shoulder, has been snapped off in a needless act of twenty-first century vandalism.

N20   SHERWOOD FOREST COUNTRY PARK AND VISITOR CENTRE

In medieval times, over one third of Nottinghamshire was covered in dense woodland some twenty-five miles in length and almost ten miles wide, which is why it's called Sherwood, derived from *Scirwuda*, meaning the shire wood. It stretched from the river Meden, which flows between Worksop and Warsop in the north, to the river Leen which curled round Nottingham Castle in the south. As a royal forest it was first named in the *Pipe Roll* of Henry I in 1130 and continued to be used by every King of England until the Tudor and Stuart period when things began to change. The forest laws were relaxed, permission was granted to clear land for agricultural purposes and the great oaks of the forest were felled in their thousands for shipbuilding and fuel for the iron industry. Great expanses of Sherwood Forest, particularly in the north – the area now known as the Dukeries – were taken from the monks and given to various aristocratic families to form the four great estates of Rufford, Welbeck, Clumber and Thoresby.

In the nineteenth century the decline of the forest increased with the sinking of coal mines as rich deposits of coal, formed from a tangle of primeval vegetation, brought massive industrialisation to the area. Small rural communities were turned into mining villages and in the last century, Nottinghamshire pits provided a large percentage of the total British output of coal. Now all trace has virtually gone.

By World War I, only 450 acres of the 100,000 acre ancient woodland remained; a few pockets of wood and heathland, chiefly around Edwinstowe. Then, in the 1950s, Sherwood Forest was made a site of scientific interest and the Forestry Commission was set up to replenish the land and a programme of planting began. The first trees were conifers that have now reached maturity and the traditional deciduous trees have since been introduced, but dotted around are still some trees of great antiquity, monster oaks that have flourished since Norman and Plantagenet times. A recent estimate placed the figure at 900 trees older than 500 years old. Many stand in majestic decay, all riven and torn and moss-grown. A lot of these are hollow and some have a bare appearance at their tops due to rotting, giving them the name of stag-headed oaks. Some of these old trees actually regenerate themselves by grafting on new growth and are called phoenix oaks.

These oaks are some of the oldest trees in Europe. An ancient heathland with woodland as undisturbed as this is incredibly rare and has given rise to a rich and complex ecosystem. This is one reason why, in 2002, Sherwood Forest was made a National Nature Reserve. It is now hard to envisage the density of the forest in medieval times, but amidst this vast world of shadowy depths and tossing verdure, the legends of Robin Hood are still kept alive at the Sherwood Forest Visitor Centre where an exhibition is devoted to Robin Hood and his Sherwood exploits. There is also a shop, information centre, tiered theatre with video presentation, activity centre, open-air theatre, and restaurant. Informative forest rangers stage interesting events throughout the year and there is an annual Robin Hood festival held here in August.

The centre was opened in 1976 to manage the quarter of a million visitors who annually walked through the woods to see the Major Oak, because everyone who knows the Robin Hood legend has heard of the Major Oak. This is the one all and sundry want to see. It was a sort of trysting place where the outlaws purportedly used to gather. It is surprising that it was not called something like

Wooden statues of Robin, Marion and the merrie men supporting the entrance canopy of Ma Hubbard's, Edwinstowe.

Left: The statue of Maid Marion and Robin Hood in Edwinstowe.

Right: The Edwinstowe sign board.

'Robin Hood's Oak'. Instead, it was named after Major Hayman Rooke, an eighteenth-century army officer and noted historian from Mansfield Woodhouse, who, in 1790, first described the tree in his publication *Remarkable Oaks in the park at Welbeck*. Prior to its renaming it was known as the Cockpit tree because, in the seventeenth and eighteenth centuries, the clearing immediately in front was used as a cock-fighting pit. It has also been known as The Queen's Oak, possibly because mature trees were given that title after that remarkable lady Queen Boadicea.

Inside its hollow belly, Robin supposedly hid from the Sheriff's men, yet this is a prime example of what gives the Robin Hood legend no authenticity. As a child I remember climbing inside the tree's hollow confines, polished over the years by the bodies of tourists. I couldn't understand how time had stood still: anyone who has ever thought about it logically realises that in Robin's day this old lady of the forest would probably have been no more than an acorn.

Estimated to be between 800 and 1,500 years old, this portly old specimen with its 30ft girth now needs a lot of support. Its rheumatic limbs are patched with lead sheets and propped with iron shackles, yet every year it sprouts new growth and a fresh supply of acorns. Visitors can only gaze from a distance: the tree was fenced off to prevent thousands of feet compacting the soil so that water could not penetrate the roots.

Although it is still marked on some maps, another famous tree known as Robin Hood's Larder has now disappeared. It was also known as the Shambles Oak, a name given to a place where animals were taken for slaughter. It is said that the outlaws used to hang poached deer and game from the upper branches so that the meat could mature before being eaten. Once a mighty tree with a hollow centre, vandals are suspected of setting it on fire and its burnt-out shell was blown down in a gale in 1961.

Other trees once singled out for special attention but now passed into oblivion had such names as The Greendale Oak (which the Duke of Portland cut a 10ft arch through), The Duke's Walking Stick (so-called for its 111ft 6ins height and straightness), The Two Porters (which held a gate between them), The Seven Sisters (seven trunks from one stool) and the Parliament Oak. Here, allegedly, in 1212, King John summoned a Parliament and with his barons laid down the conditions on which King John subsequently signed the *Magna Carta* at Runnymede.

N21 SACRED TREES AND MYSTICAL SHERWOOD

Our pagan ancestors held trees as sacrosanct, magic entities. Sacred groves were the temples of the Celts, where the Druids, an intellectual elite and ancient order of priests, performed their mysterious rituals. They worshipped nature gods, believed in reincarnation and sacrifices, and practiced their rites in forest clearings, particularly near oak trees which they held sacred.

They held annual festivals, Beltane being the ancient Celtic fire festival which took place between sunset on 30 April and sunset on 2 May. This was a festival to celebrate the return of summer, flowering and fertility. To propitiate their gods, they burnt a huge human effigy called the Wicker Man, reputedly filled with humans and animals in a ritual sacrifice. Sherwood Forest would certainly have had places where these barbaric rituals took place.

The Saxons brought with them their own pantheon of gods and do not appear to have shared with their Celtic predecessors the veneration of the tree, yet the old religion and its mysteries lingered. The Romans were indifferent to the culture and language of the people they conquered, so they were disinclined to record any detail about native religion. They assumed that these strange deities were just different guises of the gods they worshipped, and in some cases the two were merged.

When the Church came to mount its onslaught on this shadowy mythology it was to find the forests almost impenetrable, a place where a debased form of the old druidical cults still

MAJOR OAK.

An old postcard of The Major Oak before access was restricted.

persisted, yet some of these ancient practices were destined to continue in later folklore. The Beltane ceremony survived in a less barbaric form as the May Day celebrations also known as the May Games. These were the people's festivals and received no support from the Church as they were rooted in pagan fertility rites. They were considered unlawful and a profanation of the Sabbath and it was said that because of the revels and lack of religious observation, no respectable nobleman should take his wife out for fear of her chastity.

The May Games were not confined to May Day or even to the month of May and in some areas took the name of the Robin Hood Games. It was here that Robin Hood in his clothes of Lincoln green shared imagery with Hodhurst, the wood-sprite of folklore known to some as Robin Goodfellow, the Teutonic wood spirit Hudekin, and the Celtic Green Man or the Jack-in-the-Green whose carved image appears throughout Europe as a foliated head with greenery coming out of his mouth and ears.

A popular part of the May Games was the archery competitions, promoted by the popularity of Robin Hood and his dexterity with the long bow. There was no definite pattern to the games, just entertainment all day long with giants and hobby horses, morris dancers, minstrels and dancing round the maypole. Still a feature of the May Day celebrations, maypole dancing was originally conceived as a fertility dance, performed around the symbolic phallus of the maypole. One of only three permanent maypoles in Britain is set in the village green at Wellow in the very heart of Robin Hood country.

Since time immemorial, forests and woodlands have been believed to be the abode of mystical beings, places where legends persist and superstitions live on. The hollow trees called bull oaks that stand in sacred groves are believed to be the home of spirits, elves, fairies and demons. This conjures up the gentle, mystical qualities of the forest with playful spirits like Puck and Robin Goodfellow. Some of these imps are good, some are bad, so just to be sure (and in order to neutralise their magic, according to an old superstition) you are supposed to turn your coat inside out.

In *History of Nottinghamshire*, Robert Thorton captured some of these mystical elements of Sherwood Forest when he wrote 'we tread magic ground, where beings like fairies dance, where deer sport in groups unnumbered, and in limit almost unbounded; where Robin Hood and his gay followers performed their many and renowned exploits.'

What spirit has been caught on camera near this forest path?

Millions of us visit Sherwood Forest every year yet few of us actually feel that kind of magic or are tempted to wear our clothes inside out, but there are some exceptions. Andy Burroff, a forest ranger, is an expert on woodland matters but imagine his surprise when a visitor introduced himself as a witch and asked Andy to select him a suitable stick for his wand! The foresters are also aware that individuals and groups regularly practice their rituals in Sherwood Forest and celebrate the pagan festivals which mark the seasonal changes as the elements in nature die and are reborn.

The ghosts of Sherwood Forest

As well as many inexplicable mysteries, there are also ghosts to be encountered through what was once the mighty Sherwood Forest. While doing some excavation work at the Visitor Centre, a JCB driver glanced up to see a couple walking along arm in arm. A few seconds later it struck him that there was something rather odd about them: the woman was wearing a hat and the man a suit. When he looked back to check, they were no longer there. He may not have thought any more about this until a member of staff mentioned seeing a mysterious couple who appeared to be wearing clothes from the 1940s. They were walking along an old-established, though now overgrown path that was in regular use before the current hard surface paths were created, but as he watched they simply disappeared.

Of a more sinister nature, one particular area of Sherwood Forest is said to be haunted by an invisible presence. This spot induces such feelings of terror that people dare not pass it, even in daylight. It gives them the impression of being strangled. Could this be where a gallows tree stood? Alternatively, it could be a throwback to a rather barbaric Druidical practice. Human sacrifices were hung from the trees and ritually tortured so that the priests could read omens from the direction the blood spurted or ran from the wounds.

In the past, most people would agree that forests were not places to venture at night because in the wooded depths, apart from every other form of hazard and bizarre encounter, it was believed that to cross a moon shadow cast by a tree brought premature death.

As nightfall approached, it was believed that the silent ghosts of boys of an unearthly whiteness rose naked from the ground to drag any unsuspecting mortal back into the ground with them. These were said to be the spirits of children killed in the mine-workings of the forest, and the legend is based on an element of fact because, for most of the medieval period, small-scale mining took place in Sherwood Forest. In those days of bell-pits and child exploitation, it is highly possible that many children lost their lives in those early coal mines and in addition, it's possible that unsuspecting travellers also died when they blundered into abandoned, uncapped shafts.

Another tale concerning children is the English version of the Pied Piper of Hamlin. Cheated out of his fee, the piper entranced village children with his music and led them into the heart of the forest from where they were never to be seen again.

The babes in the wood legend crops up all over the place; sadly it was not a tale or a legend but a fact. Unwanted children were all too often left in the forest where their death from exposure, starvation or wild animals was a near certainty.

One particular apparition is said to wander the paths and byways of the woodlands as if searching for something or someone. He lurks in the dense woodlands where he is seen mainly at night – frequently by courting couples who park in the forest's unlit car parks. What is most interesting is that we have a detailed description of this ghostly apparition: he is said to stand 7ft tall and is of powerful build dressed entirely in green. His hair and beard are long and untidy, while his eyes are unnaturally large. Some reports claim that his eyes glow with an inner fire yet this gentle giant appears to be quite harmless. Does this make you think of anyone in particular? It's the height that gives the clue. Okay, it might have a faint echo of the Green Man, that prodigious pagan deity who stalked the forests of England, but considering the location, I'd like to think that this alarming but harmless figure is that famous outlaw Little John, Robin Hood's right-hand man.

One courting couple alerted the police after watching a huge bear ambling round the car-park. When Andy Burroff told me this story, I thought the whole thing very unlikely yet I've recently been informed that there used to be a menagerie at Thoresby Hall and amongst the animals was a mangy old brown bear. What its final fate was, no one seems to know, but one day it disappeared without trace, so to add a slight variation to the words of the old nursery rhyme 'teddy-bears picnic' – if you go down in the woods today, you could be in for a big surprise!

In 1975, Thorpe Salvin clairvoyant Simon Alexander spent two nights in Sherwood Forest in search of the ghost of Robin Hood according to a report in the 18 April edition of the *Worksop Guardian*. To make contact with the outlaw leader, he used psychometry, a form of discovery using the power of touch on inanimate objects. He went to the Major Oak and the Parliament Oak and the spirit he contacted was a Robin Hood-type character who could not give him a surname but said his name was Robyn spelt with a 'Y'. Simon described him as a smelly, unshaven creature who thought BO meant burnt oak. He was certainly not in keeping with the schoolboy's gentlemanly ruffian – more a black-hearted villain. He didn't just rob the rich, he looked for easy targets. He didn't just kill the King's deer but preferred to steal provisions from whatever source was available. He walked with a limp caused by an arrow injury to his knee and was a confirmed womaniser who had no favourites.

Other people have reported an unfriendly spirit that haunts the woods around the Major Oak. It's sensed rather than seen, and reports state that it's a strange entity that doesn't seem to have any definite form. People walking the paths around here have felt they were being followed and most visitors got the distinct impression they were not welcome. Many were so perturbed, they left in a hurry.

But don't be too disillusioned. Three clairvoyant ladies from Kent visited Sherwood Forest in the spring of 2006 and were very aware of the presence of Robin Hood who greeted them with the words 'welcome to my woods'. They were guided to a place where one of the ladies saw a group of women in medieval costume dancing round a tree. Their energy had somehow recorded and implanted itself in the ether to form a past scenario in a present-day setting. It's what is termed a time slip.

Above left: The 'babes in the wood' legend still forms a staple pantomime subject.

Above right: The outlaw Little John: is he the Sherwood ghost?

They heard the sound of horses and received a message telling them that 'we place garlands on your heads – our horsemen ride with you – our winds point you in the right direction – we watch over you – our guiding light goes with you – we are only a step behind.'

Many years previously, one of the group had made contact with Robin Hood spiritually while staying in a hotel in Nottingham. He linked in with the words, 'be my friend and I'll be yours'. She has channelled with him regularly since. For the uninitiated, channelling is a means of passing information from a non-physical being through a human medium, a form of communication between the living and the dead.

Robin told her that he was very happy in that lifetime and cared greatly about justice for the underprivileged poor folk. In complete contrast to the 1975 report, she says he's quite charming, loves to be admired and when asked which actor represented him the best he replied Michael Praed. The positive, friendly vibration lifted her spirits considerably, so at least the two different reports can agree on one thing: Robin Hood is quite a womaniser.

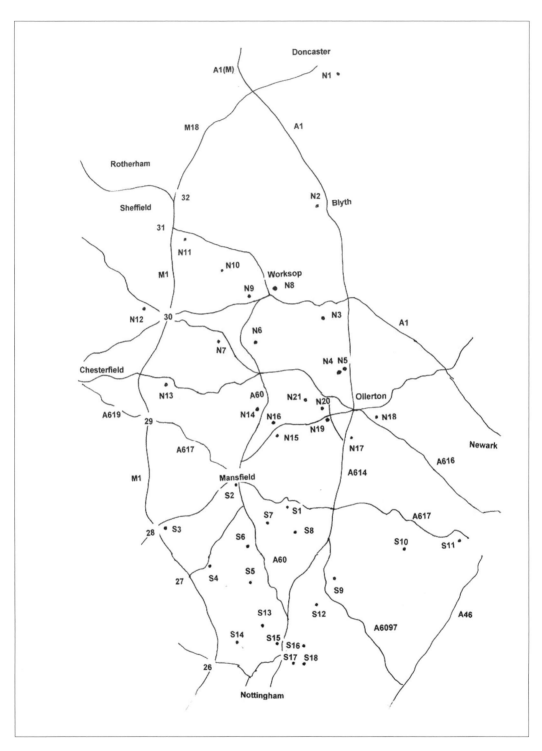

Map of the area showing key sites.

From Middle to South Nottinghamshire

Map of the area showing key sites:

Key to the map:

S1	Robin Hood's Cave at Rainworth
S2	Mansfield, the centre of Sherwood Forest
S3	South Normanton and Kirkby in Ashfield
S4	Robin Hood's Hills and Seat, Annesley
S5	Robin Hood's Stables, Papplewick
S6	Newstead Abbey
S7	Fountain Dale, home of Friar Tuck
S8	Blidworth, home of Maid Marion
S9	Robin Hood's Butts, Oxton
S10	Robin Hood's drinking flask, Southwell
S11	Robin Hood's Theatre, Averham
S12	Calverton
S13	Bestwood
S14	Bulwell
S15	Robin Hood's Cave
S16	Robin Hood's Chase
S17	Robin Hood's Maze
S18	Robin Hood's Well

SOUTH NOTTINGHAMSHIRE

S1 ROBIN HOOD'S CAVE

First recorded in 1700 as the outlaw's camp, this is a series of artificial caves built into the rocks just outside the village of Rainworth. The age of the caves is not known but they are thought to have been used as dwellings by the pre-Roman Britons. Situated in what was once the heart of Sherwood, they were quite possibly used as shelter by various outlaws during the medieval era, but caves in this area of Nottinghamshire are not unusual. Known as rock-houses, they were colonized well into the nineteenth century. In nearby Mansfield the rock houses on Ratcliffe Gate were inhabited until 1905 when the last resident Mrs Charlotte Bramwell died.

S2 MANSFIELD, THE CENTRE OF SHERWOOD FOREST

The Royal Saxon manor of Maunfeld is an ancient place that gets its name from a field by the river Maun. The Romans had a station here, and although the great camp on Holly Hill near Arnold probably contained the main body of the Roman forces, there have been Roman finds in the area and several traces of Roman roads across the forest. The road from Mansfield to Newark through part of Southwell was formerly a Roman road called The Street, and traces of this road can still be found. This would be the road along which the stone from Mansfield quarries was trundled for the building of Southwell Minster.

In medieval times Mansfield had a castle and a priory, and was set in the centre of the royal hunting forest of Sherwood. One indication of this was the name King's Stand or standing. This would have been a raised area deep in Sherwood Forest, and may have originally been a bronze-age barrow, but the term 'stand' indicates the area where a royal hunting party would wait for the game being driven towards them by beaters. Although it appeared on Ordnance Survey maps until quite recently, King's Stand is now swallowed up by a sand quarry on Berry Hill Lane, almost opposite Berry Hill Hall.

An ancient oak tree which allegedly marked the centre of Sherwood Forest stood at the end of West Gate until it was hit by a lorry in 1935, deemed a traffic hazard and felled in 1940. When the area was pedestrianised, a replacement tree was planted by Councillor Mrs Lorna Carter, chairman of Mansfield District Council, on 28 November 1988 to commemorate National Tree Week. A stone block and plaque give the details.

Will Gamwell, better known as Will Scarlet, is reputed to have been born in Mansfield. His mother was either Robin Hood's sister or aunt. Little John also purportedly lived in a cottage, long since gone, on Peafield Lane, between Mansfield Woodhouse and Edwinstowe, the site of another old Roman road.

Haunted Mansfield

Ye Olde Ramme, on Church Street, is reputedly the oldest of the haunted pubs in Mansfield. It was said to have been built before the church to provide lodgings and ale for the workmen who not only built the church, but also built a tunnel connecting St Peter's church to Ye Olde Ramme. The pub is reputedly haunted by a monk. He has been seen many times, often before a disaster or calamity, or, according to the locals, before the price of beer goes up.

S3 SOUTH NORMANTON AND KIRKBY IN ASHFIELD

Just off the M1 at junction 28 is the East Midland Designer Outlet, so stop off for some retail therapy and call in the food court where, amongst the reconstructed fibreglass medieval buildings and papier mâché forest greenery, is a splendid bronze statue of Robin Hood.

THE ANCIENT TREE WHICH GREW ON THIS SITE UNTIL 1940 WAS REPUTED TO MARK THE CENTRE OF SHERWOOD FOREST.

THE PRESENT CENTRE TREE WAS PLANTED TO COMMEMORATE NATIONAL TREE WEEK BY COUNCILLOR MRS LORNA CARTER, CHAIRMAN OF MANSFIELD DISTRICT COUNCIL ON THE 28TH NOVEMBER 1988.

A stone block and plaque now mark what was the centre of Sherwood Forest.

This retail outlet is on the site of Pinxton Castle, an old motte and bailey structure built for the Le Wynn family in the twelfth century; the ruins can be seen to the west of the main entrance road. Take the A38 to Kirkby in Ashfield. This is quite a sprawling place now but is it possible that some scribe could have misprinted Kirkby or Kirkbee as Kirklee, the place where, legend tells us, Robin died? It certainly would have made more sense for a sick man to stay on home ground instead of travelling fifty miles for 'blood-letting', so is it possible that Robin actually died and was buried at Kirkby?

S4 ROBIN HOOD'S HILLS AND SEAT, ANNESLEY

Annesley has been described as one of the abandoned villages of Nottinghamshire yet it's an ancient village recorded in the Domesday Book as Aneslei, roughly translated as the clearing belonging to Anes. It's interesting that at that time, the settlement was worth forty shillings.

Most of the area is more than 500ft above sea level and there is a remarkable assemblage of hills which are named after our famous outlaw. In fact, Annesley seems to have been a favourite spot for Robin and his men and on the top of the highest hill was a large rock known as Robin Hood's Seat. From this vantage point, the outlaw could sit and watch for likely travellers on the highway. To get an idea of how good a vantage point it was, travel into the village along the A611. Part of the road runs along a high ridge, reputedly the highest point in Nottinghamshire with tremendous views down into the valley on either side.

Apparently what made Robin Hood's rock seat so distinctive was the fact that it also had a canopy cut out of the rocks, but according to William Harrod, writing in 1801, this was destroyed around 1770 when a huge quantity of rock was cut up and taken to nearby Newstead Abbey where it was used to landscape the garden and lake.

Opposite above: The ancient tree said to mark the centre of Sherwood Forest until it was felled in 1940.

Opposite below: Mansfield's shopping centre, once the centre of Sherwood Forest.

Right: The statue of Robin Hood at the East Midland Designer Outlet.

Below: The ruins of the old church at Annesley.

The Black Monk of Annesley who haunts the area around the ruins of Annesley church.

In this area there was also a Robin Hood's Cave which, according to historian Joseph Whittaker, was cut into a sandstone outcrop. In the 1871 census for Blidworth, the recorder, Mr Clarke wrote that his father remembered the cave's destruction in the 1850s. It was used by men working on the nearby railway cutting to store dynamite; then disaster struck and all that now remains is a slight hollow or crater on the hillside.

Perhaps Robin and his men frequented this area because of the motte and bailey castle that in those days dominated Annesley and district. It has been accepted over the years that this was the ancestral home of Sir Richard of the Lee, the impoverished knight who was helped by Robin in the tale *Robin Hood and the Knight*.

Little more than the earthworks of the motte and bailey castle remain, but there is a crumbling, roofless church that Robin and his men would have been very familiar with. Behind this stands Annesley Hall, set back from the A608 and now in a sad state of repair. It has a claim to fame in its association with Lord Byron, who fell in love with the daughter of the house, Mary Chaworth, and wrote a poem, *The Bright Morning Star of Annesley*, in her honour.

The ghost of All Saints' church, Annesley

The first reference to the church at Annesley was in 1156 when it was known as Felly Chapel, and the tithes were given to Felley Priory two miles away. One of just five Augustinian houses in the county, it was attached to Worksop Priory, home of the Black Canons. In 1874, it was superseded by a new church. Slowly the ruins decayed until in the 1970s it was scheduled for demolition, but luckily the church was saved and in January 1978 listed as a Grade II ancient monument.

Just the crumbling structure of the old church now stands on a small hill, part-hidden by trees, beside the main road through the vanished village, but these ruins are haunted by a man wearing a black cloak or robe. He is most probably one of the Black Canons and is known as the Black Monk of Annesley. Passing motorists report that he crosses the road, then climbs up the hillock towards the church.

One November night in 1970, Wanda Blanchard was driving past the ruins when suddenly her headlights picked up the figure of a man crossing the road ahead of her. She automatically braked and swerved but she could not avoid him. She braced herself for the impact yet felt no bump and realised to her horror that she had driven right through him. She was understandably very shaken yet could describe the figure as wearing a dense black cowl, just like the monks of old.

To locate the church, leave the M1 at junction 27 and on the first stretch of dual carriageway, you will see the ruins over on your right. There is a pull-in in front.

S5 PAPPLEWICK

Seven miles north of Nottingham, Papplewick was one of Robin's favourite locations, near enough to Nottingham to travel there frequently, yet far enough away to avoid the constant harassment of the Sheriff's men. Here he targeted wealthy monks and bishops travelling in either direction along the King's Great Highway, a short length of which still runs just past Papplewick Hall Gates to Newstead.

Although now a private road, this was the motorway of its day along which the clergy and merchants transported money and goods, so it offered rich pickings for the outlaws. If there were any problems at Papplewick Robin had a contingency plan: he had horses stabled, ready to leave the area in a hurry.

ROBIN HOOD'S STABLES

A hidden cave reputedly used for concealing Robin's horses is still known today as Robin Hood's Stables, yet without guidance, it's as well hidden as it was in Robin's day. The cave is also on private property so permission to view, and instructions to find, must be obtained by writing to The Hermitage at Papplewick.

It's not a long or arduous trek to the cave, which is concealed in pleasant woodland 150 yards from the old highway. It could have been a medieval hermitage because it's a spacious, dry dwelling 16ft high, dug out of the soft sandstone. Our guide had a torch, but this did little to show the extend of the cave, which was certainly pitch black – it's a cave, after all – but there's not a lot to see apart from the scooped-out shelf probably used for the horse's manger or a hermit's bed. Before leaving I wanted to take a few photographs, but my flash hardly registered, so standing inside the cave I turned to photograph through the opening. When the photograph was printed, I was amazed to see a large orb inside the cave over on the right-hand side. An orb is the first manifestation of a spirit presence, so who had been in that cave with me? Just out of interest, I blew up the orb and I could see a woman's head in profile facing left.

Robin Hood's Stables, a well-hidden cave in private woodland.

St James' church, Papplewick is often referred to as the Forester's church because during the Middle Ages the wardens of Sherwood Forest were based at Papplewick. In the floor are old gravestones of past foresters, decorated with carvings of bows, arrows and the forester's hunting horn. The wardens of Sherwood would have been sworn enemies of the outlaws so it's unlikely that Robin and his men worshipped at Papplewick, although some tales say Allen a Dale was married here, a distinction shared with Stanton by Dale and Steetley.

S6 NEWSTEAD ABBEY

Newstead Abbey was never actually an abbey; it was the Augustinian priory of St Mary begun in 1163. Unfortunately all that now remains is the west front, the wall of the church that backs onto the west cloister, and the shell of the wings around the rest of the cloisters. The present chapel was the monks' chapter house and the odd room next door, in medieval times, the slype or passageway.

On an old map, following the medieval road from Nottingham to Mansfield, this area is referred to as 'Lord Byron's' and in the grounds is 'Robin Hood's Stone', obviously used as a boundary marker. A portion of this medieval road still remains between the lodge and Newstead Abbey, and the Pilgrim Tree just outside the main entrance is said to date back to medieval times. By tradition, pilgrims met under this tree before passing on to the priory.

A photograph taken from inside Robin Hood's Stable showing a definite orb.

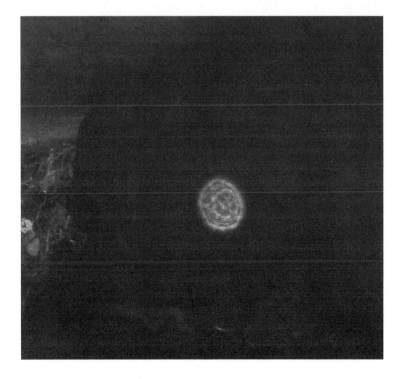

A blow up of the orb in which I can see a woman's head in silhouette.

Above: An early drawing of Newstead Abbey.

Below: A section of the medieval road from Nottingham to Mansfield. To read it turn the page and in the centre section, one third of the way up on the left of the road, is Robin Hood's Stone.

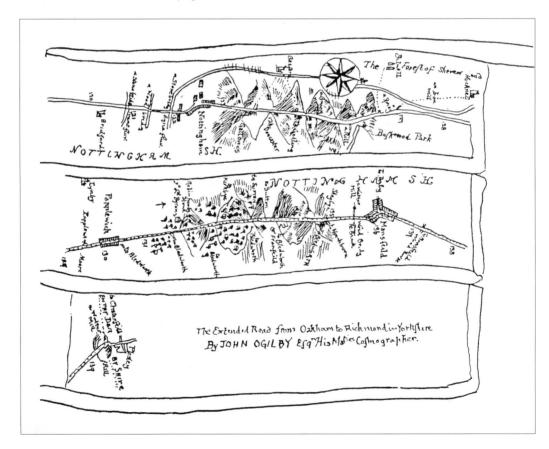

It is possible that the monastic cell at Fountain Dale, home of Friar Tuck, was attached to this monastery. Some reports say it was the monks of Newstead Abbey who placed a curse on the spring at Fountaindale, and if you think monks didn't do that kind of thing, let me tell you about the Goblin Monk; this name might seem a contradiction in terms because goblins traditionally display a malevolence to humans in contrast to the legendary caring attitude of other monks.

The Curse of the Goblin Monk of Newstead

When news of the Dissolution of the monasteries reached Newstead, the abbot gathered together all the moveable wealth and priceless documents of the house and hid them. He then conjured up a fearsome phantom that became known as the Goblin Monk of Newstead Abbey, and charged it to guard the treasure and take revenge on anyone who mistreated the abbey.

The Goblin Monk had his work cut out because, by 1540, workmen hired by Henry VIII had stripped the church of its lead roof, pillaged the buildings and generally despoiled the place. The ruined Augustinian priory was then purchased by Sir John Byron of Colwick for £810; he converted the monastic buildings into an Elizabethan country mansion. The estate passed through five successive Sir John Byrons and throughout this time, the fearsome phantom of the Goblin Monk put in a number of notable appearances. It was said that he brought misfortune to anyone who saw him yet the dissolute lifestyle led by the Byron's courted disaster.

In 1760, the 5th Lord Byron was in a boat fishing in the lake when his anchor got caught: eventually, after a lot of pulling and tugging, a large brass eagle set on a pillar of brass was hauled up. It was the lectern from the old priory, thrown into the lake by the abbot 200-plus years earlier. What was even more surprising was that the pillar unscrewed and disclosed a secret, watertight compartment in which were rare and valuable documents. The lectern was sold to Southwell Minster were it is still in regular use, but the find had obviously angered the Goblin Monk and the Byron family began to suffer a run of bad luck.

The following year, when Nottingham suffered a severe drought, the water level in the lake fell and a great chest was revealed. Surely this was the lost treasure? Lord Byron sent his servants to pull it out. They sank up to their waists in mud and thought themselves lucky to get out alive, so horses were brought and hitched up to stout chains attached to the chest, yet still it wouldn't budge. As dusk was falling, carthorses and plough teams were made ready to start at first light, yet during the night it rained and rained. Water flooded down into the lake, the chest vanished beneath the water and by dawn all hopes of recovery had gone.

The curse of the Goblin Monk continued as Lord Byron's business ventures failed and his fortunes dwindled to such an extent that he was forced to close up the remainder of the property and live in the scullery with one remaining servant. His son and grandson had died, his brother and his son too, so when the 5th Sir John Byron died in 1798 the title and wreckage of the estate passed to his ten year-old great nephew, George Gordon Byron.

Sadly the family fortunes did not improve. The 6th Lord Byron led a life of drunken debauchery and his affairs were as well-known as his poetry. Apparently the Goblin Monk was no stranger to him. While sleeping in a bedchamber known as the Rook Cell, he was woken by the sensation of something mounting the bed. Sitting up, he was confronted by a shapeless black mass, featureless apart from two red, glowing eyes; then the apparition rolled from the bed onto the floor and disappeared. Byron is also said to have seen a mysterious column of white vapour which rose from the floor and suddenly vanished without trace.

He actually wrote about seeing the Goblin-Monk although he used the experience in fiction as if it had appeared to a man called Don Juan:

Above left: The famous poet, the 6th Lord Byron.

Above right: The Goblin Monk of Newstead Abbey.

But lo! A monk, arrayed in cowl and beads, and dusky garb, appeared
Now in the moonlight, and now lapsed in shade,
With steps that trod as heavy, yet unheard;
His garments only a slight murmur made;
He moved as shadowy as the Sisters Weird,
But slowly; and as he passed Juan by,
Glanced without pausing, on him a bright eye.

The Goblin Monk took his revenge after Byron buried his dog Boatswain on the site of the abbey's high altar, and the 6th Lord Byron died of marsh fever at the age of thirty-six.

Byron had previously sold Newstead Abbey for £100,000 to Thomas Wildman, an old school friend who spent a fortune on 'doing it up'. On his death in 1860 the property was purchased by W.F. Webb, whose descendants owned the abbey until 1931 when Sir Julien Cahn bought it and gave it to the City of Nottingham as a home for the collection of Byron memorabilia that remains there.

But the Goblin Monk, or some other black-robed figure, is still seen around Newstead Abbey. One day, a man went fishing in the abbey lake with his two young sons; that evening, as he was putting his three year-old to bed, the child said, 'Daddy who was that man in the black hood who was watching us?' Needless to say, the man had seen no one but had heard the stories of the Goblin Monk.

There are many private houses dotted around inside Newstead Abbey Park. To reach them, it is necessary to take the correct branch off the main avenue through the park, not an easy job for Dr Philip Rutter when he was called out to tend to a woman in labour who lived in one of the houses in the park. 'What took you so long?' asked Mr Congdon, the anxious husband, as he ushered the doctor into the bedroom. 'I'd have been much longer if the monk hadn't pointed me in the right direction,' the doctor replied. Mr Congdon was aghast. To his knowledge, there had been no monks at Newstead Abbey for hundreds of years.

The current abbey custodian Brian Ayres is well aware of the ghostly legends and was once very sceptical about the ghostly tales until he had an experience that would change his cynical outlook forever. It was in November 1987; just another ordinary day, yet from the moment he arrived at work he had the distinct feeling that he was not alone. During the day, he busied himself with maintenance work and had just climbed onto the roof to make a routine check of the gutters when he slipped and suddenly found himself falling off the roof. He was plunging to his death, or at least to serious injury, when suddenly he felt something holding him. He scrambled back, got a firm foothold, and looked around to see what had arrested his fall. He could find nothing, not even a protruding nail, and no reason whatsoever why he had managed to avoid a 60ft drop. Perhaps when the abbot conjured up the Goblin Monk and charged it to take revenge on anyone who mistreated the abbey, the Goblin Monk also took it upon himself to look after anyone taking care of his beloved Newstead Abbey.

S7 FOUNTAINDALE

Fountaindale, on the banks of a little stream called the Rain, is said to be where Robin Hood first encountered Friar Tuck. The claim is not improbable as it is close to where there was an ancient route through the forest and, many years ago, a simple wooden footbridge spanned The Moat and a notice board proclaimed that this was the spot where Robin Hood and Friar Tuck disputed the right of way. Words led to blows and each in turn was knocked into the stream – but afterwards they became firm friends. Apparently, Friar Tuck lived there in a hermitage and baptised his converts where a chalybeate spring fed a shallow bath of water. This was known as Friar Tuck's Well.

Prior to the sale of the Fountain Dale estate in 1952, Friar Tuck's well had been surrounded by ornamental railings and covered by thick stone slabs; then an old beech tree blew down in a gale, destroyed the railings and the slabs disappeared. All that can now be seen are the stones lining the cavity of the well.

The spring periodically dries up, as do all the springs from this point westward to the stream's source near the Nottingham/Mansfield road. The valley's dryness lasts for seven years. Some reports say it's because Friar Tuck imposed a curse because of a grievance, others say it was the monks of nearby Newstead Abbey who placed the curse on this stream, but it's now dry, overgrown and barely discernible, although at times there is a low level of stagnant water.

Fountaindale Ghosts

Two families who have lived at Fountaindale House claim to have seen the ghost of Sir Walter Scott, who walks regularly through here. Clara Wilde, one-time occupier, claimed to have seen him and the present family profess to feel his presence and have had some strange things happen there.

Sir Walter Scott stayed at Fountaindale House in 1822 while he penned part of *Ivanhoe*. He called the area Copmanhurst. His hero Ivanhoe was another social rebel and freedom fighter, an almost carbon-copy version of Robin Hood, who Sir Walter Scott introduced as a character in *Ivanhoe* as Robin of Loxley.

In the valley of Fountaindale is the Blidworth Boulder, a stark, isolated stone that stands 15ft high and. is believed to be associated with the Druids and their mysterious rituals.

Left: The cavernous cellars under what was believed to be Maid Marion's home.

Opposite: The ruins of an earlier church at Blidworth.

One evening in May 1990, a local man was walking his dog. Their usual routine was to reach the stone where the man stopped and lit a cigarette while the dog scampered around searching for rabbits, yet this particular evening, the dog seemed reluctant to leave the man's side. Then the dog's hackles rose as he stood staring at the stone. The man could see nothing but when the dog started to growl in a non-too friendly fashion, he clipped the dog's lead on. Straightening up, he looked around and suddenly realised that they seemed to be surrounded by a dense, unnatural silence. A surge of unaccountable fear shot through him and he had the distinct impression that he and his pet were not alone although he could still see nothing.

Pulling the growling dog, he began to hurry home, but the dog kept turning back and snarling as if something or someone was following. The feeling of being stalked continued until they reached the first stile, when the dog's behaviour returned to normal.

S8 BLIDWORTH

Blidworth (pronounced locally Blidduth) has always been regarded as the home village of Lady Marion. In those days, the houses and cottages clustered round the main street just below the church, and she reputedly lived in a house on the site next to the present Ashfield Cottage near the Black Bull Inn. There are still the extensive, cavernous cellars which date back hundreds of years and some, disturbed in recent years, can be seen near the side of the road.

The present Blidworth church, dedicated to St Mary of the Purification, was built in the

fifteenth century to replace an earlier building, part of which is still in the churchyard. This would have been the church where Marion worshipped yet according to legend she married Robin Hood at Edwinstowe church.

There is a belief that Will Scarlet is buried in Blidworth churchyard. A rather bizarre pile of stones is pointed out as his monument. I was told that the top stones came from the previous chancel and have been placed on top of an old baptismal font turned upside down. To view Will Scarlet's monument, pass through the gate immediately beyond the water tap and it's straight ahead. Comparing its present position to a 1908 photograph taken with the church in the background, it seems to have been moved and shortened since, so don't assume that it marks Will's grave!

Blidworth would also have been a likely spot for Robin and his outlaw gang to loiter over a drink at the old alehouse where they would pick up information about travellers. It could even have been at The Bird in Hand, a Mansfield pub 100 yards from the church where the spectacular views across the valley would have given the outlaws plenty of warning of passing travellers. I would suggest parking in The Bird in Hand car park when visiting the church.

Many years ago, the cottages of Blidworth, like in many towns and villages, were tiny, two-roomed dwellings that usually housed a large family. When a family member died, it was normal practice to have the deceased laid out in an open coffin in the front parlour so family and friends could call and pay their last respects, but because many cottages were so small, it was necessary to make alternative arrangements. Many deceased were therefore laid out in the local inn and at The Bird in the Hand, it's generally believed that quite a few decided to stay. Customers regularly report a feeling of being pushed, nudged or a hand on their shoulder, yet when they turn there is no one there.

The monument to Will Scarlet in Blidworth churchyard.

S9 ROBIN HOOD'S POT, OXTON

Robin Hood's Pot is a Bronze-Age, round burial barrow situated outside the main entrance of a hill fort. It is six metres high and twenty-seven and a half metres in diameter. Another similar barrow on the edge of Sherwood Forest was opened by Major Rooke in 1789: inside was found an iron urn full of ashes of burnt bones, a large sword in a wooden scabbard, two daggers and fifteen glass beads. It was probably the tomb of a British warrior.

S10 SOUTHWELL MINSTER

Southwell (pronounced Suthl) stands proudly on the eastern edge of Sherwood Forest and derives its name from the south well which, in pre-Christian times, was seen as the abode of the gods and spirits. When Christianity displaced the ancient pagan cults, the sacred wells and springs were linked with new guardian deities; in some instances, the old gods renamed as saints, and in the case of Southwell, 'south well' became 'the Lord's well'. As a holy well, it would have been an important focus of religious activity and a place of great importance as this religious association brought the inevitable belief that the water from here could cure rheumatism. Into the nineteenth century medicine was primitive, cause and consequence of illness unknown, so holy springs offered the sick the only real chance of a cure. For many, 'taking the waters' had psychological benefit and the town attracted many visitors.

Two of the three medicinal springs in the town were within the precincts of what is often referred to as the village cathedral; the most perfect survival of an English great Norman church known as

The brass lectern fished out of the lake at Newstead Abbey.

Southwell Minster. One well was in the cloisters and one near the choir (now buried beneath the vestry, built in 1915). This well was filled in in 1764 after a clergyman named Fowler fell into it. He found that the miraculous qualities of the water did not extend to the prevention of drowning.

Southwell Minster would have been well known to Robin and his men. They would have watched the progress of the building as the imposing twin towers of the west front were erected in 1108 in creamy Mansfield stone. The outlaws would have been well aware that the forest officials of Sherwood extracted exorbitant dues from the canons in exchange for allowing them to cart their stone from Mansfield across Sherwood Forest. Little is known of the Saxon church that stood on this site, but below the 'bread pews' where the poor sat to be fed, you can see part of the floor of the previous church, covered in mosaic tiles from a nearby Roman villa.

Southwell Minster is justly proud of its superb foliated carvings and the pre-Christian fertility symbol, the green man, and here, supporting the open bible, is the eagle lectern (from the Latin *legere*, to read) fished out of the lake at Newstead Abbey after being thrown in by the abbot before the looters moved in (see the story under Newstead Abbey).

Although not on display, kept in the library at the Minster is a drinking flask that supposedly belonged to Robin Hood. It is a leather pocket flask similar in style to a Ghurkha's knife scabbard of a type popular in the sixteenth century. It was bequeathed to the minster, along with other memorabilia, by the Noble family of Southwell who could trace its authenticity back many generations.

S11 ROBIN HOOD'S THEATRE, AVERSHAM

Few villages the size of Aversham, with a population of less than 200, can boast of having their own thriving theatre, yet three miles west of Newark is the exception. It all began in 1907 when the Revd Cyril Walker became rector of Aversham and Kelham. By 1913, with the help of local volunteers, he had instigated the building of the 150-seat theatre which they called the Robin Hood Opera House. Revd Walker died in 1942 and without his enthusiastic support, interest dwindled and the opera house was closed in 1951. However, a decade later, it was re-established and officially opened in July 1961 with an ode composed for the occasion:

> Artistic creation they say knows no bounds
> A cleric named Walker who rode to the hounds
> Could preach a good sermon and painted fine scenery
> Bethought him of Sherwood and also its greenery
> So he hired him a carpenter, splendid and good
> And built him a theatre, he called Robin Hood

The Robin Hood theatre soon established regional and national links. Such people as Simon Ward, Isla Blair and Christopher Timothy began their careers there, and famous names who have appeared at The Robin Hood Theatre are Cecil Day Lewis, Michael Dennison, Dulcie Gray, Judi Dench, Anthony Hopkins and Geraldine McEwan.

S12 CALVERTON

Leave Oxton on the B6386 and head for Nottingham. At the branch of the A614 is Calverton. A spring here is said to have attracted pilgrims from far and wide in search of a new life, and tradition says that the water was so sweet, after hunting in Sherwood Forest, various Kings visited the spring at Calverton to quaff the nectar.

Calverton also has its ghosts and one I find of particular interest lurks along the winding lane that climbs up to the wooded George Hill. It's been described as a dark shape which could be male or female in a cloak. But what is most distinctive is the heavy chain or necklace hanging down on its chest. Could this be a chain of office worn by a local dignitary or even a King of England?

S13 BESTWOOD

After the Norman Conquest, William Peveril, illegitimate son of William the Conqueror, was granted immense possessions including some 162 manors spread throughout England. One of these manors was Lenton where, in 1105, he founded a Benedictine house, the great Lenton Priory. Sadly all that is now left of Lenton's once opulent and wealthy religious centre is the remains of a Norman column.

At the time of the Domesday Book, Lenton Manor included Bestwood, or as it was then written, Busckrwud – *buskr* was a Norse name meaning a thicket, and *wudu*, an Anglo-Saxon word meaning a wood. This would indicate an early settlement at the southern end of Sherwood Forest which in Robin's day would have been part of the 4,000 unfenced acres of the royal hunting forest, no doubt a regular haunt of Robin and his men.

The earliest record of a building at Bestwood dates from around 1363, when King Edward III gave instructions for the park to be enclosed and a suitable lodge built. In 1683 it was granted to Nell Gwynn's illegitimate son by King Charles II, the first Duke of St Albans. Together the teenage duke and his mother oversaw the building of an impressive hunting lodge on the estate

Right: The only trace of Robin, the first Sherwood Forester, depicted with a later recruit, in a picture panel carved in Mansfield stone and built into the wall of Bestwood Lodge Hotel.

Below: An artist's impression of the design for Bestwood Lodge, 1863.

Nell Gwynn seems to have been so fond of her time at Bestwood Lodge that she's never left.

and during this time, Bestwood had the reputation of being one of the most brilliant social centres in the country.

It remained in the possession of successive dukes, and the house built for Nell and her son was incorporated into the present flamboyant structure, built for the tenth duke in two tones of red brick and Mansfield stone. It's a rather bizarre example of a Victorian country house with oddly proportioned Gothic shapes and weird outlines that could make it rather menacing, yet it can't be taken seriously enough to be sinister.

After the death of the eleventh duke in 1934, the estate was offered for sale in 1939. It was immediately requisitioned by the Army and remained in military use until the 1970s. Now Bestwood Lodge is a hotel that is full of character, open to residents and non-residents alike and quite a remarkable 'find'.

The ghosts of Bestwood Lodge Hotel

While researching, I found that the most prolific spirit presence at Bestwood Lodge Hotel is a lady dressed in the fashion of the seventeenth century, who is often seen walking through the grounds. She is not a quiet ghost; she laughs and chats to invisible companions as if in the happiest of moods. Unsurprisingly this is believed to be the shade of Nell Gwynn enjoying the afterlife as much as she enjoyed her mortal life. Nell seems to have been so fond of her time at Bestwood that she has never left.

Prior to becoming an actress and the King's mistress, Nell gained notoriety as an orange seller, and the smell of oranges is often reported here, 300 years after her death. I was looking for confirmation/denial of this, and asked the barman about the unexplained aroma of oranges. He readily confirmed that visitors and staff still frequently reported this in the King Charles' suit. At the time, we were sitting under the lofty glass dome in the grand hall with its first floor arcaded galleries off which are the bedrooms.

'And what about the monk that has been seen in front of this fireplace?' I asked. 'Not sure about a monk,' said my informant, 'but the other week, one of those vases filled with flowers fell off the fire surround, and there was no reason why it should.' I turned to look at the ponderous stone fireplace he was indicating.

It would need a step ladder to get up to the level of the vases, unless they overbalanced or were knocked by some floating phantom. 'Perhaps the flowers were unbalanced and simply fell over,' I suggested, but he slowly shook his head. His silence said more than words.

THE SHERWOOD FORESTERS

Built into an outside wall of Bestwood Lodge Hotel is a picture panel carved in Mansfield stone depicting Robin Hood and a Sherwood Forester. The Sherwood Foresters are the old established infantry regiment of Worcestershire, Nottinghamshire and Derbyshire. In the *Historical Record of the Royal Sherwood Foresters* by Captain A.E Lawson, published in 1872, he wrote:

> At Agincourt in 1415, the Nottinghamshire Archers again played a prominent part, and there for the first time on record, they fought as Sherwood Foresters. Their banner was quaintly described by Drayton as:

> 'Old Nottingham, an archer clad in green, under a tree with his drawn bow that stood
> Which in a chequered flag far off was seen; it was the picture of bold Robin Hood.'

Since 1965, Nottingham Castle has housed a collection of artefacts of the Worcestershire and Sherwood Forester's Regiment.

S14 BULWELL AND ROBIN HOOD'S WELL

On its way to Mansfield, the King's Great Highway ran between Bestwood Park on its east, and Basford and Bulwell on its west. The name Bulwell is derived from a well or spring that no longer survives, although water from the spring now fills a pond at a nature reserve at Moorbridge.

Of several explanations given for its name, the most quixotic is the one about the bull. This great, wild creature roamed through Sherwood Forest until, one day, he found his way blocked by a large boulder. In his rage, he attacked the boulder, knocked off a chunk and from the fissure poured clear spring water. A hamlet grew around the spring and was given the name Bulwell. Amongst the stone picture panels built into the outside walls of Bestwood Lodge Hotel is one depicting the legend of the Bulwell Spring.

At Beauvale, not far from Hucknall, is the scant remains of a once influential Carthusian priory, the only house of this order in Nottinghamshire, and the site of another Robin Hood's well. Because it supplied the priory with water for both domestic and holy purposes, it gained the reputation of being holy water, and its ice-cold water was considered by some people to be an aphrodisiac as well as having healing properties. Robin Hood's Well is situated in High Park Wood behind the priory ruins, but both these sites are on private land with no public access.

S15 ROBIN HOOD'S CAVE

Heading towards Nottingham, take the A60 Mansfield Road to the Forest Recreation Ground. This was once part of Sherwood Forest known as the Lings. It was not a dense mass of trees, but a sandy wasteland with scrubby bushes and a few hardy trees. In a primitive state of cultivation for centuries, animals both wild and domestic grazed the area bisected by ancient paths cut by centuries of passing feet.

The Lings were a resource for the people of Nottingham, a centre for sports and shows, and gentlemen and nobility used the Lings to race their horses. The earliest racecourse was four miles long, shortened in stages over the years to one mile. Racing at the Lings ended in 1890 but at one time, Nottingham's races ranked alongside those at Newmarket, York and Ascot.

Underneath this area of Mansfield Road are enormous caves dug out over centuries. The sandmen who mined here went round the Nottingham streets shouting, 'lily white sand-o, who wants some lily white sand-o?' and housewives bought it for scattering on floors and for use as an abrasive cleaner.

Adjacent to the Lings is Church Rock Cemetery, built into the sandy hillside, and amongst all the graves are three large cave formations with graves lying on top of and around them. These are known as Robin Hood's Caves. They would no doubt have been a convenient hiding place for the outlaws just outside Nottingham.

In days gone by, the area near the entrance of the Church Rock Cemetery was known as Gallows Hill. It was a large area of open ground because hangings were well-attended public spectacles. In one of the Robin Hood tales, Will Scarlet, or in some versions Will Stutley, was captured by three varlets hired by the Sheriff, thrown into Nottingham prison and was to be hung high on the gallows the following morning. As a last request, he asked to be given a sword and let him fight until he was killed, but the boon was not granted as the crowds were waiting expectantly. In an era when trials and punishment were often the only form of entertainment available to the peasants, these occasions qualified as a half-day holiday. They were administered in a sort of carnival atmosphere. Trinkets and mementoes were sold, jugglers and clowns entertained while vendors sold fruit and snacks. Even for petty theft, punishable by a day in the stocks or pillory, the crowd amused themselves throwing rotten vegetables at the culprit.

Fortunately, Will was rescued on Mansfield Road as he was about to be taken to these gallows; the last person to be hanged on Gallows Hill was William Wells, for highway robbery, on 2 April 1827.

S16 ROBIN HOOD'S CHASE

Being a short distance from The Forest Recreation Ground, Robin Hood's Chase could have been part of the original racecourse that covered four miles, or it could have been named after the ballad of that name in which Robin Hood leads the King a merry chase from London and back to London via Nottingham, York, Berwick, Carlisle and Lancaster.

Robin Hood's Chase is a main street in the St Anne's district of Nottingham, a finger-like valley about two miles long which juts away from the city northwards. The valley is bounded on the north, west and east by hills of bunter sandstone and in the lower area of the valley there were a great many natural springs where the water gushed up and formed small streams. In medieval times, much of this area was thickly wooded country within or adjacent to Sherwood Forest; then, during the sixteenth and seventeenth centuries huge quantities of trees were felled until, by the nineteenth century, there were only woods at the far end of the valley.

Until the early part of the nineteenth century St Anne's was not heavily populated: then, as the population of Nottingham soared, St Anne's was built over with low-cost housing. In the

Robin Hood's Cave in Church Rock Cemetery.

1970s much of the district was demolished because it was deemed to be a slum area, but it has since been extensively redeveloped.

S17   ROBIN HOOD'S RACE

Leaving Robin Hood's Chase and driving up Well Road; on the left is The Shepherd's Race filling station, a reminder that many years ago, just behind here, was The Shepherd's Race also known as Robin Hood's Race. This had no connection with the Forest Racecourse or horses; the name was given to a turf maze, cut in the ground and constructed in the same way as a large-scale labyrinth:

> a rut within a grass plot, deeply cut and wide enough to tread
> to tire the feet, perplex the mind, yet pleasure heart and head

They were called Shepherd's race, run, hey or ring because from as far back as the Bronze Age, and perhaps even earlier, shepherds cut into the turf or leys to produce them.

The object of the turf maze was to test your dexterity by starting at the outside and negotiating the narrow path without crossing the boundaries until you reached the centre. This was no mean task when you consider that Robin Hood's Race occupied a piece of land only eighteen yards square, yet through its intricate windings, the path was five hundred and thirty-five yards in length. The design of this maze was distinctive because of its horseshoe projections facing the four cardinal points.

Some historians stress that the maze was originally created not for amusement but as a penance, the work of the monks at St Anne's Chapel. Penitents were ordered to follow the

Robin Hood's Race.

sinuous course on their hands and knees, to repeat prayers at fixed points and more when they reached the centre. On average this took over an hour, and as the path was scarcely a foot wide and gravelled, this was penance indeed.

Many superstitious folks believed that these turf mazes were the haunts of fairies and one villager in 1908 said he had often walked the maze on a summer's evening and knelt at the centre to hear the fairies singing. These curious mini-mazes were still common in the English countryside less than a hundred years ago although the original Robin Hood's Race was ploughed up in February 1797 when the area was turned over to farming. It would appear that another maze was constructed about 1838 in Poynter's Tea Garden, a public tea garden at the top of Blue Bell Hill, on a site which overlooked the valley of Robin Hood's Well and could not have been far from the original maze.

It was an amusing test of dexterity to tread its intricate paths, but the star attraction was a clipped poodle dog belonging to the establishment who ran the race and was rewarded with a halfpenny which he carried to the house and exchanged for a dog biscuit. The maze was probably destroyed when the old house was pulled down about 1860.

S18 ROBIN HOOD'S WELL

It is not surprising that the main road running through this area of St Anne's is named Wells Road. Here in previous centuries a great many natural springs gushed up from the ground and one of interest that stood at the bottom of Ransom Road was called the Rag Well. The water here was credited with curing eye complaints and the name came from the practice of soaking a rag in the water, bathing the eyes, then hanging the rag on a bush to dry. It's not clear whether this was part of the cure, i.e. as the water in the rag dried the problem eased, or the rag was a communal cloth guaranteed to spread infection throughout the area.

But the well I was interested in was Robin Hood's Well, alias Saint Anne's Well, which was originally known as Oswell or Owswell, now situated in the backyard of the Gardener's Inn, Wells Road. The name Owswell has led to speculation that it could be derived from Robert Fitz Othe, the Earl of Huntingdon who is believed by many to be Robin Hood, but it was certainly known as Robin Hood's Well for many centuries.

THE MAZE NEAR ST. ANNE'S CHAPEL.
From a Drawing by Mrs. Robert Miles.

Penance in Robin Hood's Maze, St Anne's Chapel.

There is a document in the private collection of a Mr McJohnson which states that 'Robin Hood and his marauders were charged with causing an affray at Owswell'. The date given was 1195 when William Brewer was Sheriff and held pleas in Nottinghamshire and Lincolnshire. Apparently Robin and his men only avoided prosecution when a Lincolnshire nobleman, Robert de Kyme of Lindsey, Lincolnshire made a plea in court on behalf of the outlaws and the charge was dismissed. If this is genuine, it's rather surprising that there is no ballad story of the incident.

The earliest information we have about Owswell is that it was linked to a hermitage so it was considered a holy well due to the healing properties of the water. Unfortunately there is no documentation as to which monks resided at the hermitage. King Henry IV (1399-1413), who frequently visited Nottingham, is known to have taken the waters at Owswell as a possible cure for his leprosy, and in 1409 he gave money to the monks of the hermitage for a chapel to be built and dedicated to St Anne, the patron saint of wells, springs and married women. Tradition says St Anne was mother of the Virgin Mary.

Around 1543, the hermitage and chapel were adapted by the corporation for secular use after the Dissolution of the monasteries, and when a connection was made between the well and that brawl with Robin and his men, it was renamed Robin Hood's Well. In 1617, the hermitage and chapel were replaced by a house of refreshment on a lavish scale and during the seventeenth century it became the practice for the mayor, aldermen, local dignitaries and other town officials, accompanied by their retinue, to parade here on Easter Monday. These social outings with lavish entertainment continued until the Civil War when such pomp and ceremony was frowned upon.

During the seventeenth and eighteenth centuries, Robin Hood's Well was one of the most popular tourist attractions and even enticed royalty. When the throne of King James II was tottering in 1688 with the invasion of William of Orange, his younger daughter Princess Anne fled to Nottingham with her husband Prince George of Denmark. She stayed until 1702 when she returned to London to become Queen of England, but during her time in Nottingham, the princess regularly visited Robin Hood's Well to take the waters. At the time, and possibly because of her patronage, many believed that the waters helped women conceive. She married in 1683

The water at Robin Hood's Well used to rise into a little pool and formed a small stream.

but, despite numerous pregnancies, all her children sadly died in infancy and on her death in 1714 the rule of the House of Stuart came to an end. Another connection with Queen Anne: in Castle Gate is an inn named The Royal Children because, according to tradition, her children were accommodated there during this time.

As an added attraction at the well site, local tradesmen sold souvenirs and displayed what they claimed were relics of Robin Hood: his arrows, his cap, his chair and his gravestone which, if not donated by the Armytage family of Kirklees, was a fair copy. In 1700, diarist James Brome in his *Travels over England* described a jocular initiation ceremony at the well. 'Placed in the chair, we had a cap, which they claimed was his, very formally put upon our heads, and having performed the usual ceremonies befitting so great a solemnity, we received the freedom of the chair, and were incorporated into the society of that renowned brotherhood.'

The water used to rise into a little pool covered by an artificial cave, but in 1797, John Throudy described the well as 'under an arched stone roof of rude workmanship and steps leading down into the water'. This would indicate that it was used as a bath despite being described as 'water so cold it would kill a toad'.

Due to the rowdy behaviour of its clientele, the house of refreshment (obviously of the intoxicating type) had its licence withdrawn in 1825 when a tea room took over the running of the well. The so-called relics were sold in 1827 to an actor named Mr Raynor who took them to London where they were used in various melodramatic theatrical productions, and eventually, it is believed, they were presented to the British Museum, though that prestigious establishment claims no knowledge of them.

Above: The ornamental Gothic well house that stood over Robin Hood's Well.

Below: A sketch of the derelict property at St Anne's Well.

The tea room closed in 1855 and on 19 November 1855, the town council voted to have the house and buildings at the well site demolished and the spring bricked up to prevent access to the water. They may have had good intentions when they commissioned Mr Tarbottom, a local architect, to design and build an ornamental, gothic well-house to commemorate Robin Hood's Well, but sadly the effort was in vain. In 1887, the Tarbottom structure was demolished when the Great Northern Railway was built and the site was excavated to a depth of 30ft for the foundations of the north abutment of the railway bridge. The railway company offered to present the monument to the town for erection elsewhere but their offer was refused by the council, so the monument, instead of preserving a site of great antiquity, suffered the same sad fate.

The well's location was lost for many years then with the closure of the railway line in 1987 it was located at the rear of The Gardeners public house in Well Road. There is absolutely no visual evidence of this on the tarmac surface of the featureless back yard, yet if the well could be re-established, the site would convert perfectly into a beer garden. At the moment, the only evidence of its existence is a plaque on the side of the building proclaiming that this is the site of St Anne's Well, buried in 1887.

Nottingham Centre

NOTTINGHAM

Enter Nottingham on the A60 Mansfield Road and you will pass York Street where, behind York House, is the only surviving reminder of the ancient **KING'S GREAT HIGHWAY.** Robin Hood purportedly hid or stabled his horses on the site of York Street, in order to make a fast getaway.

Shire towns such as Nottingham had a defensive wall around them and as you pass the Victorian Shopping Centre and enter the city of Nottingham, you are about to cross Upper Parliament Street which is where the town walls once ran. Part of the wall, originally 30ft high and 7ft thick, was discovered here when the railway was being laid through Nottingham. It's now in the castle grounds.

Continue down Clumber Street until you reach the Council House, Exchange Building and **ARCADE**, built by Cecil Howitt in 1920 in classical style. Note the impressive domed

Above left: The fresco of Robin and his band in the Exchange arcade.

Above right: A statue of Robin outside Nottingham Castle.

cupola, then go inside, locate the cupola and look up. It's 200ft high under the dome which is 28ft in diameter. In each of the four spandrels, you will see impressive frescos (paintings done directly onto plaster) by two local artists Noel Denholm Davis and Hammersley Ball. Each fresco marks a great event in Nottingham's history: the Danes capturing the town, William the Conqueror ordering a castle to be built, Charles I raising his standard and Robin Hood with his outlaw gang. To get Robin's stance as a bowman correct, the artist took archery lessons. He modelled the figures on local celebrities and borrowed the faces of Albert Iremonger, the 6ft 4ins goalkeeper of Notts County Football Club, for Little John and Mrs Popham, wife of a local doctor, for Maid Marion.

While here, you might hear the chime of the hour bell of the 9ft clock, hung 200ft up in the dome of the adjoining Council House. It is one of the loudest and deepest toned (E-flat) bells in Britain and on a good day it can be heard seven miles away. It has a similar tone to London's Big Ben, but this is Nottingham, so this ten-ton bell is named **LITTLE JOHN**.

Wander outside into **THE OLD MARKET SQUARE**, the heart of the city. This was originally the town green where the Sheriff held those famous archery contests. Robin would have competed here on many occasions. Those early fairs were the predecessor of St Matthew's Fair held annually on 27 September, later renamed the Nottingham Goose Fair and moved to the Forest Recreation Ground, near Robin Hood's Caves in Church Rock Cemetery, where it is still held today.

In 1155, King Henry II granted Nottingham a charter to hold a twice-weekly market in the Market Square, and it was here that Robin, disguised as a potter, sold his pots (or, as a butcher, his meat). On the west side of the Market Square is Beastmarket Hill. Here stands **THE BELL INN**, one of the three contenders for the title of the oldest inn in Nottingham. It is believed that The Bell Inn was built around the refectory of an old Carmelite friary that could possibly have been the original home of Friar Tuck. The main passageway has the original flagstones along which travellers led their horses to the stables at the rear of the building The cellars date from Norman times with a small cave reputed to be Anglo-Saxon.

Because of its religious connection, the original inn was called The Angel. The ancient fabric of the old Angel Inn remains untouched and when the pub is quiet, an unseen phantom sings gently to herself. When one of the neighbouring shops was undergoing refurbishment in 1969, the workmen accidentally broke through into what had been a cave or cellar that had been blocked up for many centuries. It's not sure which property the chamber belonged to, but soon after, the ghost of a man dressed in a long, dark coat and wearing a wide-brimmed hat began to be seen in the street. No one knows who he was and he is still seen, so watch out!

From Beastmarket Hill continue back along Wheeler Gate, pass St Peter's church, which probably dates from around 1180, then wander between the courtyards or turn into Albert Street, Low Pavement and continue until meeting **FLETCHER GATE**. Fletcher Gate is now a main thoroughfare running north from the Broadmarsh Centre, yet it still retains its name from the days when this street housed the workshops of the bowyers (bowmakers) and fletchers (arrow makers). Tradesmen built their workshops at the front of the building where they and their families lived.

The wood to make an arrow would need to combine strength and lightness and black poplar was especially good. Each shaft or stele would be between 27-35 inches. One end held the flights made of goose (or peacock feathers for the rich), stuck on with pitch and tied with silk or linen thread. The other end had an iron arrowhead made by the local blacksmith and attached with glue made out of bluebell bulbs.

Our next location is **ST MARY'S CHURCH**, where Robin went to pray in *Robin Hood and The Monk*. The Saxon church of St Mary's was recorded in the Domesday Book of 1086, incorporated into the Norman church which was built over in 1474 giving us the late medieval building you see today as you enter the world-renowned Lace Market area.

In the original ballad, Robin was very restless and came to St Mary's church in Nottingham where he was recognised by a monk he had formerly robbed of £100. The monk alerted the Sheriff, Robin was captured and thrown into the dungeon under Nottingham castle, and the monk rode to London to get an execution warrant from the King. But help was at hand. The monk was waylaid and replaced by Little John, who obtained the warrant and returned to Nottingham castle. The Sheriff declared a celebration, got roaring drunk and passed out, giving Little John the opportunity to slip down into the dungeons and rescue Robin.

But just suppose that this was done with the help of the Sheriff's wife: what if the reason for Robin's restlessness was because he was planning an assignation with his lover? If she had been late for her appointment and arrived as Robin was being arrested, she could have ridden into Sherwood Forest on that little white horse he gave her in *Robin Hood and the Potter*, to raise the alarm. She could have made sure that Robin's incarceration in the castle was made more bearable, and at the celebratory feast, drugged her husband's wine to give Little John the opportunity to release her lover.

Let's follow in the footsteps of Robin Hood, who was dragged from St Mary's church to Nottingham Castle, so backtrack across Fletcher Gate, down Low Pavement and turn left into Castle Gate, one of the four medieval streets which ran from the castle to the marketplace. Continue to the end of this section of Castle Gate where it meets Maid Marion Way and on

St Mary's church, where Robin Hood was arrested by the Sheriff.

your left is **ST NICHOLAS' CHURCH**. The present building was constructed in 1671 on the site of a very much older church, founded about the time of the Norman Conquest (1066). Robin Hood is said to have used St Nicholas' as a hide-out.

St Nicholas' graveyard previously stretched over the area that's now Maid Marion Way, so when this fast dual carriageway was being constructed, understandably many graves were disturbed. Amongst them were mass pauper's graves, the bodies being buried without ceremony or identification. Some were re-interred, but supposedly many unidentifiable bones were piled up awaiting a decision as to what was to be done with them. It was at this time that the workmen began experiencing strange phenomena. They heard sinister voices calling their names, tools disappeared and reappeared days later in an entirely different place, ditches refilled themselves overnight and the men reported feeling uneasy, as if many pair of eyes were watching them. A decision was made to remove the bones, and rather than waste this free supply of calcium, they were ground up and incorporated into the concrete of what is now Lloyds TSB building.

On the opposite side of Castle Gate is **YE OLDE SALUTATION INN** where the Nottingham Ghost Walks begin every Saturday evening. This inn, built *c*. 1240, got its name from the Annunciation of the birth of Christ by the Angel Gabriel to the Virgin Mary and is also known as 'Archangel Gabriel Salute the Virgin Mary'. It may have originally been the guest house for the Carmelite or White Friars on Beastmarket Hill.

The building is ancient, but the cave system underneath was in existence long before a building was ever thought of. Here, the cave's design and construction, with a 70ft well sunk through the rock, would have been an ideal spot for an early cave settlement. In AD 868, Asser, biographer of Alfred the Great, wrote of Nottingham being called 'Tigguocobanc' or 'House of Caves'. Most of Nottingham lies on soft, Bunter sandstone, sedimentary rock laid down millions of years ago and going down to

200ft. Generations of troglodytes have scooped themselves homes in it. It's surprising that there is no mention of Robin taking his mattock, shovel and mallet and digging himself a des. res. town house, but perhaps that would have been too close for comfort to his arch-enemy at the castle.

In 1336 when Edward III stayed at Nottingham castle, many of his retinue were housed and fed at 'Ye House By Ye Sign of Salutation.' In 1642 when Charles I raised his standard at Nottingham the inn was used as a recruiting office. During the coaching days, the house had a sinister reputation as it was frequented by highwaymen so it is not surprising to find a number of resident ghosts in a place like this, but there is no sign of Robin Hood.

In one of the cave's alcoves sits a teddy bear left for Rosie, a four year-old street urchin who once lived in the caves and has stayed there in spirit form ever since. It could be Rosie who regularly plays pranks in the inn, or perhaps it's the ghostly highwayman, or a previous landlord who also haunts the place. Glasses move, ashtrays lift and levitate, keys disappear and glasses fall off shelves but float for several seconds before crashing to the ground.

Cross **MAID MARION WAY**, described as the ugliest road in Europe and an insult to Maid Marion, and resume your journey on the other section of Castle Gate. This was once the red light district, but we'll not go there.

Straight ahead is **NOTTINGHAM CASTLE** and the dry outer moat where in pride of place now stands the 7ft **STATUE OF ROBIN HOOD**, sculpted by James Woodford and presented to the city by Philip Clay, a local businessman to commemorate the visit of Princess Elizabeth and the Duke of Edinburgh on 28 June 1949 during the city's Quincentenary Celebrations.

Robin is cast in eight pieces of half an inch thick bronze, weighs half a ton and stands on a base weighing two and a half tons. Compared to our modern day superheroes who are tall, slim and fit, this figure is rather short and stout which has earned it the nick-named 'the world's largest gnome'.

This area is a very popular tourist attraction and no self respecting visitor would leave without having their photograph taken with Robin as he sturdily draws an invisible bowstring, because unfortunately, our medieval outlaw is no match against twenty-first century vandals and souvenir hunters. Without his bow string and arrow, poor Robin stands there in a strange boxing stance, so a bit of imagination is needed.

Dotted around are reclining **STATUES OF SOME OF THE MAJOR FIGURES IN THE OUTLAW BAND** – Little John is repairing his bow, Friar Tuck is reading, Will Stutely is reclining, and Allen a Dale plays a harp to Will Scarlet. Bronze plaques depicting events in the legends of Robin Hood are set into the castle walls around this area.

Turn round and across the road you will see a remarkable medieval merchant's house dating from 1450. Its original address was 10 Middle Pavement, but the building was moved to this site 'en bloc' when the Broadmarsh Shopping Centre was built in 1969. In its original position it was a restaurant known as the **HOUSE OF SEVERN**; now it is the Lace Centre, devoted to the history and sale of the world-famous Nottingham Lace, where demonstrations of hand-made lace making are still shown.

Walk down the hill to **THE TRYPPE TO JERUSALEM INN**, hewn out of the rocks beneath Nottingham Castle. The Tryppe, an Old-English word for halt or gathering place, was built in 1189, the year of the ascension of King Richard the Lionheart. He crusaded against the Saracens who at the time occupied the Holy Land, so it's possible that this inn would have been a watering hole for knight's going to the Crusades. It's also reputedly the oldest inn in England although in Nottingham alone it shares that distinction with The Bell and Ye Olde Salutation Inn. The Tryppe was originally the brewhouse for the castle and there are still the remains of a speaking tube between there and the castle.

Robin Hood may have indulged here too, so can you visualise it as it was then? This tavern would have been a hotbed of gossip and the customers would have been entertained by ragged minstrels who wandered round fairs, markets, wayside inns and anywhere they could attract a paying audience. In order to get the attention of the audience, a minstrel might start with something like the opening lines of *The Lytell Geste of Robin Hood*: 'lythe and listen gentlemen that be of frebore blode/ I shall you tell of a gode yeman, his name was Robyn Hode'. But that was then, and now, rather than tell you one of the Robin Hood stories, I'll tell you a few ghost stories associated with this quaint city pub instead.

Firstly, this place has atmosphere. It's a cross between an inn and a museum and the walls and ceilings are hung with all manner of artefacts, some dating back to the Civil War. The lighting casts weird shadows and it's easy to imagine you've seen something that shouldn't be there. Sometimes a waft of perfume fills the air, a scent which the landlady describes as old-fashioned. A clock hanging in the bar is said to be possessed by a spirit and the two Dobermans of a previous landlord would stand and bark at it for no reason.

Once you've got yourself a drink, go up to the Rock Lounge as that seems to be a focal point for odd happenings. This haunted snug is a cosy little room that sits above an unused basement area and has been used at different times as a shop and bedroom. Staff have heard the sound of breaking glass in here but been unable to find any when they went to clear it up, keys disappear, then turn up again in odd places, and bottles fly off the shelves and smash. A previous landlord named Yorkey, who held the licence from 1894-1914, is believed to be still haunting the inn, so is it him?

Right: The statues of Will Scarlet and Allen a Dale outside Nottingham Castle.

Opposite: A costumed guide appears to be in the flight path of Robin's arrow outside Nottingham Castle.

The most bizarre phenomenon at Ye Olde Tryppe to Jerusalem is associated with an old ship – now in a glass case complete with dust – hanging from the ceiling of the Rock Lounge. It is one of several ships said to be gifts from sailors when Nottingham was an important inland port situated on a stretch of the River Trent navigable to the sea. Some sailor would have made this ship to while away the time he was at sea, but who he was is a mystery and will remain so as no one dares wipe the ship to look for a name. According to reports, the last three people who cleaned it died mysterious and unexpected deaths within twelve months. Locals understandably say it is possessed by an evil spirit who ensures an untimely end for anyone who touches it, so during the inn's renovation in late 1997, a local spiritualist was called in to move the ship and cast a spell protecting the inn and its occupants.

Interconnecting caves shared with Nottingham Castle are used as cellars and a ghostly woman wearing what has been described as a crinoline dress has been seen walking down the steps into these cellars. A group of tourists asked if they could go and explore them but beat a hasty retreat when confronted by two Roman foot soldiers who walked toward them and then passed through a wall. There is an entrance to Mortimer's Hole (see the castle's ghost stories) where previous landlords have seen a man and woman, and heard people calling when there was no one there. Some reports say you can smell tallow candles burning down there.

But by far the worse place is the condemned cell of the castle prison where a curious green mould grows on the walls and ceilings, but there is something more to the cell's oppressive

Opposite: Four reliefs showing Maid Marion helping Robin and Friar Tuck in their fight against Guy of Gisbourne's men; King Richard the Lionheart joining Marion's hand with that of Robin; Robin and Little John fighting on the bridge, and Robin shooting his last arrow.

Right: The Severn building, a medieval merchant's house.

atmosphere than its natural chill. When two of the pubs regulars, full of Dutch courage, decided to spend the night there, they lasted twenty minutes and were violently sick afterwards.

Just below the castle is Fishpond Drive running parallel to **CASTLE BOULEVARD**. In Norman times, this area was honeycombed with caves that were the homes of an important group of religious hermits. They may also have harboured Robin Hood because according to *The Life and Times of Robin Hood as seen through the eyes of the Robin Hood Society* (1977), a boy sleeping in a Cave House overlooking Fishpond Drive saw the ghost of Robin Hood here.

Nottingham Castle stands on its 133ft rock, although anything less castle-like is hard to imagine. What happened to that chunky, impregnable stone castle that the name conjures up? Emrys Bryson, in his book *Portrait of Nottingham*, suggests selling it the Americans and replacing it with a proper castle that lives up to the expectations of the thousands of disappointed visitors that flock to see the stump of a romantic castle complete with towers and turrets and decaying dungeons. Perhaps someone should lay siege to this seventeenth-century structure, but the only arrows that now point in its direction are on the sign posts.

The original castle would have been a wooden structure on top of the same high crags, surrounded by a palisade of wooden stakes and a moat. Curling round its base to the South was the River Leem, diverted by the Normans and diverted again to flow into the Nottingham and Beeston canal when Castle Boulevard was constructed more recently. In the time of Robin Hood the castle was one of Prince John's headquarters and in 1170, Henry II gave money for the building of a stone castle to replace the old wood and earth structure. This early medieval castle was destroyed during the Civil War, so that was the end of the mighty fortress that had overawed the Midlands for 600 years. In its place, in 1679, this Palladian-style palace was built by William Cavendish for the sum of £14,000 at the same time that he was building Bolsover Castle. Incensed rioters set it ablaze in 1831; it lay in disuse for forty years but was then restored in 1875 when the corporation acquired the lease. The Oxford University Trust acquired the building, which was sold in 1952 to the city of Nottingham for £16,000.

Pass through the great stone arch of the restored but feasibly ancient gatehouse where the rattling chains of the portcullis once clanged and a drawbridge creaked ominously beneath the weight of heavily armoured knights. It's almost possible to imagine the clink of swords as they charge out of the guard rooms, but now this houses a souvenir shop and a special display about

An artist's impression of what Nottingham castle could have looked like in the days of Robin Hood.

Robin Hood and his men. Walk up to the castle where, since 1965, a collection of artefacts of the Worcestershire and Sherwood Forester's Regiment has been housed. Recent excavation work has uncovered parts of the original castle that are now open to the public and it is possible to go on a guided tour of the castle's tunnels and caves that honeycomb the rock on which it stands. These caves were used as dungeons where many prisoners were incarcerated. In *Robin Hood and the Monk*, Robin was captured and thrown into the dungeons under Nottingham castle, but Robin Hood escaped from his captivity.

In 1212, twenty-eight boys, some as young as twelve, from Welsh noble families were not so lucky. They were taken hostage by King John and kept at Nottingham castle until their execution. Despite their pleas for mercy, one by one they were taken up onto the ramparts and hanged in a row. They say that their pitiful cries, pleading for mercy, can still be heard within the castle precincts.

These subterranean caves and tunnels are known to be very haunted, especially the famous tunnel known as Mortimer's Hole, named after Sir Roger Mortimer, Earl of March. His ghost is said to wander along the subterranean passages looking for a way to escape. Mortimer was the paramour of Queen Isabel, wife of the gay King Edward II, and it was believed that together they had plotted his murder. At least that's what her son Edward III thought, because on the night of 19 October 1330, while Sir Roger and Queen Isabel were staying at Nottingham Castle, he planned to take his revenge. With a band of supporters, he entered the castle through a series of secret tunnels, probably from Ye Olde Tryppe to Jerusalem, burst into his mother's bedroom and dragged Mortimer away down the same route.

The gatehouse of Nottingham Castle.

Queen Isabel pleaded, 'Fair son, have pity on the gentle Mortimer,' a cry that is purportedly still heard echoing around the empty tunnels, but the plea fell on deaf ears. Mortimer was hanged, drawn and quartered on 29 November 1330.

No trip to Nottingham would be complete without a trip through **THE TALES OF ROBIN HOOD,** so opposite the castle gatehouse, head back down Friar Lane and turn left along the busy Maid Marion Way. The window frontage gives a tantalising glimpse of what can be expected inside and as the whole experience is undercover, it's one for a rainy day.

The Tales of Robin Hood is a modern telling of the outlaw's story, launched in March 1988 using high technology to produce sights, sounds and smells that bring the past to life. In the comfort of electric cable cars, you travel through medieval Nottingham passing reconstructed buildings based on historical evidence and even incorporating medieval stonework from demolished churches. The sets consumed thirteen and a half miles of electrical cable, 137 tons of concrete, 600 bags of plaster and 1,200 sheets of plasterboard. The reconstructed Sherwood Forest has 250,000 leaves on the trees, all dyed and wired by hand, and the overall effect is a triumph for the artists and craftspeople responsible.

Staffordshire

LOXLEY

Robin was born in Locksley or Loxley as it is often spelt, but there is some confusion about the county. Some say Nottinghamshire, some say Yorkshire, or could it be Loxley in Warwickshire or in Staffordshire? It has been assumed over the years that the Loxley referred to is in Yorkshire, yet there is evidence that it could be Loxley near Uttoxeter in Staffordshire.

If Loxley in Staffordshire was Robin's birthplace, it would also be the place of his juvenile exploits. It is near to Tutbury and Doveridge, both places mentioned in *A new Ballad of Robin Hood showing his birth, breeding, valour and marriage at Titbury (Tutbury) bull-running.* Despite the title this ballad gives very little help in establishing where Robin was actually born because it states that Robin was born in Locksly town in merry Nottinghamshire, but there is no trace of a Locksly ever being in Nottinghamshire although that is not conclusive proof that such a place never existed. The number of names of towns and villages of which there is now no trace would fill a volume.

The ballad says his father was a forester; his mother was niece of a Coventry knight, Sir Guy, Earl of Warwick and sister of George Gamwell of Gamwell Hall, Nottinghamshire, and that's about the full extent of his family tree. Robin meets Clorinda who is on her way to Tutbury fair: he joins her and they ride 'five Stafforshire miles', but before they have reached their destination, he has asked her to marry him, the parson of Doveridge is called and joins them in marriage. The obvious question here is, didn't Robin Hood marry Maid Marion at Edwinstowe?

Although most people accept that Robin is buried at Kirklees, some historians have tried to re-link him with what they consider to be his ancestral home at Loxley in Staffordshire. Apparently in the churchyard adjacent to the north wall of the village church is a grave slab identical to the gravestone drawn by the Pontefract antiquarian Nathaniel Johnston in 1665, and published in Richard Gough's 1786 book *Sepulchral Monuments of Great Britain*, as being the grave of Robin Hood. Could this be the actual gravestone that Johnston drew, not the one sited at Kirklees as people assumed? Although the church was certainly standing in Robin Hood's lifetime, unfortunately no burial records survive, and it's doubtful that any inscription chiselled in stone can weather more than a few hundred years.

A bow which, it was claimed, belonged to Robin Hood was on display at Loxley Hall in Staffordshire. During the Second World War, the hall was used as a prisoner of war camp and during this time, some American troops stationed there removed it – permanently. What was believed to be Robin Hood's Horn, won at an archery competition, was also at Loxley Hall until the hall was purchased by Staffordshire County Council and converted into a school.

The horn, mounted with silver ferrules and suspended from a silver chain, was engraved with ornamentation, the initials R.H, and three horseshoes in a shield, the arms of Thomas de Ferrers of Loxley Hall. Could he be another contender for the title of Robin Hood?

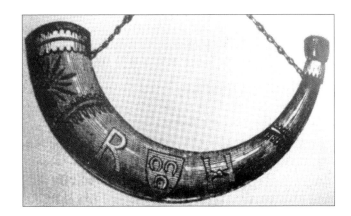

Right: Robin Hood's horn.

Below: Robin Hood blowing the horn.

Derbyshire

The county of Derbyshire is not normally associated with Robin Hood, yet just inside the Derbyshire/Nottinghamshire county boundary at Renishaw Hall is Robin Hood's bow; there is a hamlet named after him, numerous geological features and at Hathersage, on the Derbyshire/Yorkshire border, is Little John's Grave.

D1	Robin Hood's Bow at Renishaw Hall
D2	Robin Hood's Hamlet
D3	Robin Hood's Leap
D4	Robin Hood's Stride
D5	Robin Hood's Marks
D6	Robin Hood's Picking Rods
D7	Robin Hood's Chair
D8	Robin Hood's Cross
D9	Robin Hood's Pricks
D10	Robin Hood's Well and Little John's Well
D11	Hathersage
D12	Robin Hood's Stoop
D13	Robin Hood's Cave

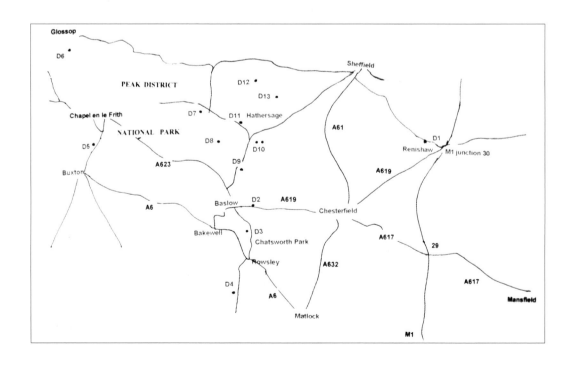

D1 ROBIN HOOD'S BOW
Because the bow is at Renishaw Hall, which is just inside the Derbyshire county boundary, it has been given a Derbyshire reference, but the story is covered in the North Nottinghamshire section.

D2 THE HAMLET OF ROBIN HOOD
On the A619 a mile from Baslow is a hamlet called Robin Hood. There is a Robin Hood plantation, Robin Hood Farm and Robin Hood Pub. Many pubs were named after Robin and it was not uncommon to find these little ditties displayed in a prominent position of welcome:

> You gentlemen and yeomen good,
> Come in and drink with Robin Hood
> If Robin Hood be not at home
> Come in and drink with Little John
> OR

> My beer is stout, my ale is good
> Pray stay and drink with Robin Hood
> If Robin Hood abroad has gone
> Pray stay and drink with Little John

D3 ROBIN HOOD'S LEAP
A deep gorge in Chatsworth Park has been given the name Robin Hood's Leap because Robin is said to have leapt over it as he was anxious to get away from the Sheriff's men. This is also the name of a Derbyshire ballad found in *The Life and Exploits of Robin Hood* (Milner and Sowerby, Halifax, 1859). The tale is about a lady called Kitty Ray who lived at Edensor, the estate village in Chatsworth Park. She protected Robin Hood in a delightful love story, but there was no lasting relationship and each went their separate way.

D4 ROBIN HOOD'S STRIDE
Travelling along the road from Alport to Ashbourne, I was told that after one and a half miles, I'd see the silhouette of the rock outcrop known as Robin Hood's Stride over on my right. 'You can't miss it,' I was told, 'it's also known as Mock Beggar's Hall because its silhouette resembles a building with two chimneys.'

After travelling a few miles, it was obvious that the silhouette wasn't as obvious as I'd been told and I had missed it. I could see a rock formation but there were no distinctive two chimneys on the skyline.

Leaving my car, I started my trek, stopping at intervals to check whether the 'chimneys' had mysteriously appeared. They hadn't but it gave me a regular excuse to stop and get my breath. The rock formation seemed shrouded in trees that blurred the outline, so I kept climbing anxious to see whether it would be different from the top. It wasn't but it's quite an invigorating upward stride for anyone walking to the top of this Derbyshire landmark.

The view from the summit is pretty remarkable and I could see Robin making use of this elevated spot as a lookout point, but the local legend tells of something much more worthy of note. Apparently Robin stood with one foot on each of the 'chimneys' and urinated into the valley below. Nine maidens passing were so shocked they were turned into stone. From my elevated vantage point amongst the rocks and trees, I looked round for the nine stones hewn roughly into human form. I didn't expect to find any detail but I wanted to see standing stones or at least stones that had once stood. There weren't any. In a way I was pleased. After all, Robin Hood was a gentleman. He wouldn't have done that kind of thing … or would he? It's such a lonely spot – who would expect to find nine maidens passing just when you are answering a call of nature?

To find Robin Hood's Stride, go to Rowsley, three miles south of Bakewell, and take the road to Youlgreave, branch at Alport, go one and a half miles until reaching a pull-in. Park, cross the road and take the drive on your right marked footpath and head for the hills.

D5   THE ARCHER'S WALL and ROBIN HOOD'S MARKS

The *Lay of the Buckstone* is a Derbyshire ballad of the High Peak, in which a fight takes place between Robin Hood and keepers of Peak Forest. It mentions the men marching up from Fairfield side, a large village near to Buxton, beneath the Archer's Wall. In a 1797 map of the parish of Chapel-en-le-Frith, part of the ancient Forest of the High Peak, I traced this old wall which is still a boundary on Coombs moss. Although it is named on the map the Archer's Wall, the length of it is traditionally called Robin Hood's Marks.

D6   ROBIN HOOD'S PICKING RODS

Two stout, stubby monolithic relics of antiquity that were once called the Maiden's stones. They stand close together and are set into one massive stone base. They are unmatched, both short and rounded but one shorter than the other. They are probably the remains of two pillar crosses marking the intersection of boundaries as they apparently stand at the crossing of two old tracks near Glossop.

The name Robin Hood has suggested the theory that they may have been used for stringing bows. Such a device would have been useful for bending the bow while attaching the cord.

D7   ROBIN HOOD'S CHAIR

Mentioned in one of Professor Child's *English and Scottish Popular Ballads*, this is a rock formation sited in the Hope Valley.

D8   ROBIN HOOD'S CROSS

In olden days, every boundary was traditionally identified by a name, a marker stone or wayside cross, but as they are no longer of any use, most have now disappeared. One of the very earliest place names recorded in 1319 refers to Robin's Crosse in the Bradwell area of the Peak District, three miles west of Hathersage. There is no cross there today, but to reach the site, turn up the steps by Bradwell church and take the steep hill track over Bradwell edge and Abney Moor.

D9   ROBIN HOOD'S PRICKS

Elias Ashmole, born in 1617, wrote a mid-seventeenth century manuscript that is now at Oxford. In it he refers to Robin Hood's Two Pricks, near Grindleford Bridge. Translated, it states, 'Little John lyes buried in Hatherseech Church yard within 3 miles fro Castleton in High Peake with one stone set up at his head and another at his feet, but a large distance betweene them. They say a part of his bow hangs up in the said Church. Neere Grindleford Bridge are Robin Hoods 2 Pricks.'

D10   ROBIN HOOD'S WELL AND LITTLE JOHN'S WELL

Just north of Grindleford on the Longshaw Estate, two wells named after Robin Hood and Little John drain Totley moor. To locate them, take the A625 Sheffield/Hathersage road, branch right

The silhouette of Robin Hood's Stride.

onto the B6055 to Hathersage and on your left is the Longshaw Estate. Over to your left at the Y junction is Little John's well. Take the left fork and Robin Hood's well is on the right.

D11 HATHERSAGE

Many people visit St Michael and All Angel's church, Hathersage to see the grave of Little John. The present church dates from 1381 but there was certainly evidence of a Norman church on this site. But why is this Little John's final resting place? Some people say he was born in Hathersage and returned to die, a scenario I find rather unlikely. Hathersage is in the remote Peak District, which in Robin Hood's day would have been very wild, almost totally isolated and a million miles from Sherwood Forest.

After Robin's death, Little John probably never forgave himself for letting his master die without realising that treachery was afoot. He probably left Kirklees and went off to live as a hermit as penance or to avoid the wrath of the other members of Robin Hood's band. Alternatively, bearing in mind that he had just lost his best friend and constant companion, with no one to issue orders or make decisions, Little John was probably totally lost in more ways than one and wandered aimlessly around until he reached Hathersage where he collapsed from exhaustion.

Could these be the petrified nine ladies at the foot of Robin Hood's Stride?

According to the stories, he predicted his death, dug his own grave and gave instructions that he was to be buried without a coffin or shroud. As the ballad says:

His bow was in the chancel hung, his last good bolt they drove
Down to the nocke, its measured length Westward fro' the grave
And root and bud this shaft put forth when Spring returned anon
It grew a tree and threw a shade where slept staunch Little John.

The grave which lies in the churchyard just opposite the main door has huge yew trees at each end, so could one of these have sprouted from Little John's 'last good bolt'? The grave is a simple earth mound with three stone slabs; one at the head, one at the foot and an earlier headstone on its length. On the latter, it is just possible to trace the carved figure of a stag but the writing is almost indecipherable. The whole is surrounded by a low enclosure of metal railings erected by the Ancient Order of Foresters in 1929.

Little John's grave was opened in 1728 and bones of an enormous size found in it. In the late eighteenth century it was opened again by Captain Shuttleworth, brother of the squire of the parish, and according to a 1784 report by the Revd Charles Spencer Stanhope, the local vicar,

Handwritten extract from Elias Ashmole's manuscript.

a thigh bone 32ins long was exhumed and put on display by Captain Shuttleworth. Believing that it had brought him bad luck, he gave it to the parish clerk to arrange for it to be reburied, but the clerk kept it in his window with a notice explaining whose bone it was. Supposedly Sir George Strickland took it from there and all further traces of it have been lost.

In 1847, the last occupant of the cottage where Little John died was seventy year-old Jenny Shard. The cottage had been handed down through the family for generations. She remembered the grave being opened by Captain Shuttleworth, and the thigh bone being taken into the cottage and measured. In keeping with his last wish, Little John's bow hung in the chancel of Hathersage church until 1729 when it was taken for safe keeping to Cannon Hall, Cawthorne near Barnsley.

On the Derbyshire/Yorkshire border in the remote area above Hathersage are a number of sites bearing the Robin Hood name although with the area's connection with Little John, it seems unfair that his name doesn't appear instead. **ROBIN HOOD'S STOOP (D12)** is purportedly the site where Robin and Little John once stood and shot an arrow over a mile to land in Hathersage churchyard, while north of Hathersage is **ROBIN HOOD'S CAVE (D13)** a fissure in the granite crags of Stanage Edge that lie at the edge of the moors to the west of Sheffield.

Little John's Grave.

This 700-year-old slab may have marked the original grave. The inscription is faint but still traceable, and it's now in the church porch, to preserve it from further weathering.

HERE LIES BURIED

LITTLE JOHN
THE FRIEND & LIEUTENANT OF
ROBIN HOOD
HE DIED IN A COTTAGE (NOW DESTROYED)
TO THE EAST OF THE CHURCHYARD
THE GRAVE IS MARKED BY
THIS OLD HEADSTONE & FOOTSTONE
AND IS UNDERNEATH THIS OLD YEW TREE

The current headstone on Little John's grave at Hathersage.

Yorkshire

To aid continuity, let's begin our Yorkshire journey just north of Hathersage at what is considered by some to be the birthplace of Robin Hood.

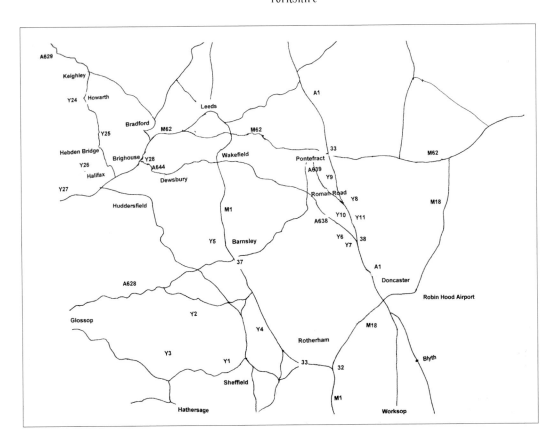

Y1 LOXLEY

In the anonymous prose of the Sloan manuscript (*c.* 1600) in the British Museum, Robin's birthplace is recorded as Locksley (now Loxley) in Yorkshire. To support this, both Roger Dodsworth and antiquarian John Harrison (writing in 1637) stated that a house at Loxley Chase called Little Haggar's Croft was where Robin Hood was born. Apparently, it stood on a hillock near a duck pond and a stream flowed down the far side.

A photograph published in the *Sheffield Telegraph* in 1937 showed an oak beam encrusted with remains of bracken with which the roof had been thatched. It was reported as having been part of Little Haggar's Croft. Apparently, in 1887, a forestry expert had declared it had grown in the woodland nearby and was 1,000 years old (there was no carbon dating then). The whereabouts of the beam are now untraceable and in about 1970 a new housing estate was built on the site of Little Haggar's Croft.

Y2 BOLSTERSTONE

As old sites disappear, new sites and discoveries still occur. About five miles north of Loxley, experts from Sheffield University have just started a preliminary dig at the site of an eleventh-century castle in the village at Bolsterstone, South Yorkshire. They believe it was the home of Waltheof, the Earl of Huntingdon, a Saxon who strongly opposed the Normans and is a likely contender for a forefather of Robin Hood.

Mr Haldane holding what is believed to be Little John's longbow, which measures at least 6ft 7ins.

Y3   ROBIN HOOD'S MOSS
Part of the High Peak Moorlands, north-west of Sheffield, overlooking the Derwent Dams.

Y4   ROBIN HOOD'S WELL
Situated five miles north-west of Sheffield at Low Hall Wood, north east of Ecclesfield.

Y5   CANNON HALL, CAWTHORNE
Cannon Hall at Cawthorne near Barnsley is now a museum yet, as a private dwelling, it was here that, according to Ritson, Little John's Bow was brought in 1729. Colonel Naylor, a relative of William Spencer of Cannon Hall, is recorded as the last man to string the bow and shoot a deer with it. It bears the name Naylor with the date 1715.

The bow was made of spliced yew and tipped with horn, weighed 2lb and needed a pull of 160lb to draw it. The length of the bow reputed to be 6ft 7ins long (most longbows were 5ft long) is supposed to coincide with the height of the person using it, so at a time when the average height of a man was around 5ft 4ins, Little John would appear to be over 6ft 7ins. A photograph taken outside Cannon Hall of a Mr H.C. Haldane holding Little John's bow shows the length in comparison to the height of a normal man.

Staff at the museum remember the bow hanging in the hall in the late 1960s when it was a private residence prior to the death of the last owner of the hall, Mrs Elizabeth Frazer. On her death, the bow was given to the Wakefield museum, but staff say it was then taken to a manor in Scotland by Mrs Frazer's son, Mr Simon Frazer, who died in 2004.

Y6 HAMPOLE

The action in the earliest written stories of Robin Hood, *The Lytell Geste of Robin Hood*, takes place around Barnsdale in South Yorkshire. It is generally accepted that the author set it there because he was familiar with the topography and locations of that area, so if my theory is correct, Richard Rolle was responsible for writing those early Robin Hood ballads. It's also acknowledged that the author was writing after the lifetime of our outlaw and Richard Rolle was a fourteenth-century mystic, a saint and a prolific writer.

Richard Rolle, also known as the Hermit of Hampole, was the first man to write in the English vernacular language of the time, an achievement which in itself should be enough to secure him a place amongst Yorkshire's greatest. Most of our major libraries contain some of his writings and many of his poems and ballads were later printed by Wynken de Worde. Richard was born at Thornton-le-Dale in East Yorkshire. He was accepted into Oxford at fifteen, yet dropped out to become a hermit, living beside the Cistercian nunnery/priory of St Mary at Hampole, a tiny hamlet just off the A1, about seven miles north of Doncaster. Here he devoted his life to prayer and to his writings which were much sought after, read and copied.

He died and was buried on 29 September 1349 at Hampole, but after his death his fame increased, Hampole became a place for pilgrimage and a number of modest miracles followed. Like all such establishments, Hampole Priory was a casualty of the Dissolution of the monasteries, fell into disrepair and disappeared; the site was excavated in a modest way in 1937 and a report states that the greater part of the remains lie under the village green. Now, all that can be seen on the site is a monument to Richard, the Hermit of Hampole, who could have sat on this very spot and written those early stories that until then had only been passed down verbally.

Y8 BARNSDALE AND BARNSDALE BAR

In the *Geste* and other early ballads, Robin is referred to as Robin of Barnsdale, a twenty-five square mile, forested area lying between Doncaster and Ferrybridge in South Yorkshire. Barnsdale was not a royal forest bristling with officials and it had no great castles or important settlements. It was a tract of woodland extending from the North of Doncaster to the River Went, and from Badsworth on the west to Askern on the east. Hampole lies almost in the centre, just off the A1 (junction 38) which cuts through the middle of Barnsdale in the path of the Great North Road.

In a manuscript dated to around 1600 in the British Museum's Sloan Collection – referred to as the Sloan manuscript – Robin and his men are said to have 'haunted about Barnsdale Forest'. But it's not just Robin and his men. This area does seem to have an historical reputation for outlaws and bandits. In 1307, the King paid the fee for escorting the Bishop of St Andrews and the Abbot of Scone from Scotland to Winchester. According to the report, eight archers accompanied them down to Pontefract, where they were joined by another dozen archers as far as Tickhill, 'on account of Barnsdale'.

Leland, on his rounds in Elizabethan England, saw 'the woods and famous forests of Barnsdale where they say that Robin Hood lived like an outlaw'. Sir Walter Scott wrote in *Ivanhoe* of a forest that could be medieval Barnsdale, where 'hundreds of broad headed, short stemmed, wide branched oaks flung their gnarled arms over the thick carpet of the most delicious green

sward. In some places they were intermingled with beeches, hollies and copse wood of various descriptions, so closely as totally to intercept the level beams of the sinking sun.'

Barnsdale Bar, a term that usually referred to a barrier or gate to impede travellers, is today the busy junction 39 at the intersection of the A1 and A639 the old Roman road to Pontefract.

Y9 WENTBRIDGE AND SAYLES

Early Robin Hood ballads refer to 'Wentbreg' (Wentbridge), the bridge over the River Went where the outlaws would wait for wealthy travellers two miles north of Barnsdale Bar. Wentbridge was the medieval crossing place and in the ballad, Robin Hood and the Potter, Robin encounters the potter at Wentbridge. There is still a picturesque, stone bridge over the river, probably enclosing an earlier medieval structure. This mainly eighteenth-century bridge carried all traffic until bypassed in 1965 when a high viaduct was constructed half a mile downstream from Wentbridge to carry the fast, incessant traffic of the A1 over the valley.

In the opening verses of *The Lytell Geste*, Robin instructs Little John to 'walk up to Sayles and so to Watling Street and wait for some unknown guest.' Watling Street was the name of the Roman Ermine Street which passed west of Pontefract while the Great North Road took a more easterly route. The name Sayles is still given to a plantation in the village of Wentbridge, yet there seems to be some confusion as to whether this was the original site referred to in the ballad. Some say the intended site was in the region between Robin Hood's Well and Robin Hood's Stone, on the banks of the River Skell, because Salix is the name given to the willow *genus*, and Crack Willow (*Salix fraglis*) grows on both banks of the River Skell. The Osier Willow (*Salix viminalis*) was introduced by the Normans; its supple stems are exceptionally suitable for basket making, and Skelbrook, which takes its name from the River Skell, had osier beds where

Right: A commemorative blue plaque, sited on the bridge at Wentbridge, giving a brief history of Robin Hood in this area.

Opposite: The monument to Richard Rolle on the site of Hampole Priory.

willow was collected to make baskets, a widespread cottage industry when baskets were needed for marketing, fish-traps, lobster pots and bird cages.

Y10 ROBIN HOOD'S STONE

The oldest surviving record of a Robin Hood landmark comes from Yorkshire's Monk Bretton Priory near Wakefield, where a deed of 1422 mentions a Robin Hood's Stone, marking a field boundary less than a mile to the south of Barnsdale Bar. This boundary stone and guide post lay to the west of the road sited in a field at Sleep Hill, between the villages of Skelbrook and Wrangbrook.

Henry VII travelled up from Doncaster with an impressive retinue and was met by the Earl of Northumberland and a great and noble company in Barnsdale, 'a little beyon Robin Hood's stone', a comment that holds great significance. Many people fuse Robin Hood's Stone and Robin Hood's Well, yet I believe the two, although in the same vicinity, were definitely separate locations as this comment would indicate.

Y11 ROBIN HOOD'S WELL

Sited on the east of the road (not the west like the stone) by the side of a stream called The Skell, a spring bubbled up then disappeared under the old Roman road. It was not given the name Robin Hood's Well until much later, yet it was a convenient meeting place and halt along the Great North Road. It would appear that it was also the centre of an early Robin Hood-related tourist trade, because it became a regular stopping place for the stage coaches from London to York. Here travellers paid to hear the local legends and tales of Robin Hood, drink the well water and purchase souvenirs.

The picturesque stone bridge over the River Went at Wentbridge, the medieval crossing place where Robin and his men would wait for wealthy travellers.

It was probably officially named Robin Hood's Well when, in the seventeenth century, a canopy designed by the architect John Vanburgh and commissioned by the Earl of Carlisle was built over the well. In 1727 there was the possibility of the canopy supporting a statue of Robin Hood and Little John, and although Lord Harley proposed to supply a statue, he did not carry out his plans.

Two inns stood here – The Robin Hood, which kept sixty horses in reserve, and the New Inn, favoured by lower-class workers such as cattle drovers. In the heyday of the coaching era, this road was traversed daily by thirty coaches, plus heavy luggage and fish wagons.

As a child, a man who was born at a cottage near the well recalled being taken there to draw water for domestic use. He remembered the water being fresh and ice-cold until the local coal mines were sunk. That polluted the water, which was then condemned. Now all that remains of Robin Hood's Well is the stone canopy because the stream was diverted during road widening, so the well is now dry and stands at the end of a lay-by on the south-bound carriageway of the A1. It can be seen clearly from the north-bound carriageway, yet it is inaccessible due to the central reservation and crash barriers, so continue up to junction 39, Barnsdale Bar, to cross the motorway, proceed south and pull into the lay-by almost immediately after the road to Burghwallis.

YORKSHIRE'S WELLS

A dependable supply of water was essential to any community so it's not surprising that the places where a spring bubbled up and a well was formed were identified as places of great importance and given names. That's why there are numerous wells in Yorkshire that have been named after Robin Hood and Little John, yet a sad consequence of the development of piped water is the neglect and loss of many of these old wells. It's a loss of our cultural and social heritage as much as to the communities they once served.

There is a **LITTLE JOHN'S WELL (Y7)** beside the road to Wakefield near Hampole where a spring bubbles out at the base of the west facing magnesium limestone scarp. In North East Yorkshire, two miles north of Danby in the North Yorkshire Moors National Park is a **ROBIN HOOD'S WELL**, and **ROBIN HOOD'S BUTTS**, three tumuli on Danby Low moor **(Y18).**

The canopy of
Robin Hood's Well.

There is a **ROBIN HOOD'S WELL**, one mile west of Kirkbymoorside, and in the same vicinity, is **ROBIN HOOD'S HOWL**, a hollow or hole on a southern escarpment on the edge of the North York Moors **(Y13)**.

One and a half miles from Halton Gill near Pen-y-Ghent in the Yorkshire Dales National Park and almost directly on the Pennine Way is another **ROBIN HOOD'S WELL (Y22)**. Pen-y-Ghent is 693ft above sea level and one of the highest points around. Still in the Yorkshire Dales National Park, one and a half miles north of Threshfield, there is another **ROBIN HOOD'S WELL (Y21)**. Further south, there is a **ROBIN HOOD'S WELL** near to Stornbury **(Y24)**, two miles west of Howarth on Keighley Moor.

This selection of wells gives some indication of just how many Robin Hood's Wells there are in Yorkshire. Unfortunately not all these are now operable and I'm sure there are many more that have now faded into oblivion.

It's not just wells that bear the name of the famous outlaws. In Yorkshire there is a hamlet named Robin Hood, one mile north of Catterick Bridge, along the old Great North Road **(Y19)**.

There is **ROBIN HOOD'S PARK (Y20)**, four miles south-west of Ripon in the area of Fountains Abbey, and **ROBIN HOOD'S BED (Y27)** which is part of the ridge called Blackstone Edge in the Pennines, five miles north-east of Rochdale.

In Holden Park, an ancient deer forest between Keighley and Skipton, is **ROBIN HOOD'S STONE (Y23)** and there used to be **ROBIN HOOD'S PENNY STONES**, one at Wainstalls **(Y25)** and the other at Midgeley Moor **(Y26)** in the Pennines, close to Hebden Bridge. These were two immense stones weighing several tons each and probably druidical monuments. They acquired the name Robin Hood's Penny Stones because Robin is reputed to have thrown them for fun, probably in the way a Scotsman would toss a caber. One story says that Robin stood close to the Standing Stone near Sowerby and threw the great stone that landed at Wainstalls, five miles away on the other side of the Calder Valley. Country people around here will tell you that he disturbed the other stone while digging and threw it off an adjoining hill. There is now no evidence of either of the stones, which were reported to have been broken up by road menders.

The traffic of the A1 viewed through the arch of Robin Hood's Well.

The impressive ruins of St Mary's Abbey in the Museum Gardens, York.

Y12 YORK

A very popular Yorkshire city complete with its ancient city walls intersected at intervals with towers, one of which is named after our hero. There is no evidence that Robin ever came to York yet Little John did, acting as knave to Sir Richard of Lea when he repaid the money owing to the greedy abbot in the ballad *Robin Hood and the Knight*, which features in *The Lytell Geste*:

> Then spoke that gentyll knyght
> To Lytel Johan gan he saye
> To morrowe I must to Yorke toune
> To Saynt Mary Abbey
> And to the Abbot of that place
> Foure hundred pounds I must pay;

In Robin Hood's day, this Benedictine house, the home of the infamous greedy abbot and cellarer, would probably have been the most important and influential monastery in the north of England. Now this abbey church is an impressive ruin in the Museum Gardens, a delightful park on the banks of the River Ouse just inside the city walls at the end of Lendal, the pedestrianised shopping area, a short walk from York Minster.

The main structure stands tall and serene amongst the neatly cut lawns, and scattered around it are stunted columns, blocks of stones and footings with name plaques giving the visitor an idea of the layout and scale of those early monastic buildings.

Y14   THORNTON-LE-DALE

The birthplace of Richard, the Hermit of Hampole who very probably wrote the first stories about Robin Hood. Thornton-le-Dale is on the A170 road to Scarborough, Robin Hood's Bay and Whitby, a stretch of coastline familiar to Richard and featured in the early tales. Thornton-le-Dale is also about the same distance from York, so is it possible that Richard viewed the clergy of that age with such animosity that he singled out the greedy Abbot of St Mary's, York, who seems to have been well known for his uncharitable hypocrisy, to feature in *The Lytell Geste*.

Y15   ROBIN HOOD'S BAY

There are few settlements along the rocky coastline between Whitby and Scarborough, yet halfway along is Robin Hood's Bay with its labyrinth of twisting streets and red-roofed cottages crammed together in a little declivity of the cliffs perched dramatically above a sweeping bay.

It's been known as Bay Town, Robin Hood's Town and when first mentioned in Leland's description of the town in 1538, Robbyn Huddes Bay. It gained notoriety for the smuggling that was carried out here over many centuries, so it's surprising that no one wrote a tale entitled *Robin Hood and the Smugglers* because there is *Robin Hood and the Viking Pirates* set near Whitby, and *Robin Hood and the Noble Fisherman* in which Robin worked as a fisherman out of Scarborough.
There are several legendary theories about the origin of the name. One affirms that the Abbot of Whitby Abbey asked for Robin's help in fighting off Danish invaders. Robin did this by hurling large boulders and other missiles down the cliffs to crush the attackers and as thanks, he was allowed to keep a boat here for when he needed to get out of the country. Who knows, Robin Hood could have started the smuggling racket that has sustained this small community for centuries.

Although fishing was the more legitimate activity and main livelihood, smuggling, or 'free trade' as it was known, was a well-organised activity in the bay. They say that the closeness of the houses linked attics, cellars and adjoining cupboards for passing goods, while tunnels and secret doors meant that goods could pass from shore to cliff top without seeing daylight.

Like Robin and his outlaws, smugglers may have been regarded as rogues and thieves, yet because they defied what many regarded as unjust taxation, they were accepted and even admired by a large section of the population. Perhaps this is one reason for the name of the bay – Robin Hood would have felt very much at home here involved in these illegal activities. He would have enjoyed pitting his wits against the Customs inspectors in the same way he taunted the Sheriff of Nottingham.

The ghosts of Robin Hood's Bay

It's not surprising to find that one of the ghost stories of Robin Hood's Bay originated in those early days of smuggling, and even today some people will not walk up Linger's Hill after dark in case they meet Linger's ghost. This white-sheeted figure (usually a local farmer) riding a white horse appeared in the area when a smuggling run was due as it was desirable to scare inquisitive snoopers away.

But there are also the 'genuine ghosts'. Old Bert Marshall was a farmer at Robin Hood's Bay and one of the meanest men around: he'd never spend money on anything but beer and rather than have a set of false teeth made, he acquired those of a dead neighbour. Then disaster struck as Old Bert was stumbling home along the railway track drunk one night, and next day his headless body was found. A train had obviously severed his head from his body. The head had disappeared and was never found, so now, according to legend, the headless spectre of Bert Marshall wanders around the area searching for his missing head, one arm outstretched, the other hand clenching the false teeth that he periodically clashes like a castanet.

In 1780, the cottages along King Street, the village's main road, fell into the sea and in 1792, another part of the road with more cottages followed. But this is nothing new. This coastline has been subject to erosion for centuries and chunks of land periodically fall into the sea taking with it whole villages whose ghostly church bells still toll under the waves. There are tales of phantom Roman armies marching far out to sea along long-vanished roads, and last century, a local fisherman named James Harrison fell 600ft to his death, and now his ghost is frequently seen hovering in mid-air about 20ft out to sea.

Y16 ROBIN HOOD'S BUTTS

This is where Robin and his men allegedly practiced with their longbows. Legend says that they shot towards Robin Hood's Bay, about a mile away, thus giving it the name. Many towns and villages had places called butts. Originally they were the border lands that butted up to boundaries, then they became the area where archery practice was carried out, taking the name from the target. Here, Robin Hood's Butts are actually three mounds, 775ft above sea level, south of a beacon at Stoupe Brow. One of the mounds was excavated in 1771 and found to be an ancient burial site.

Y17 WHITBY

Whitby is an atmospheric coastal town with historical associations as diverse as Robin Hood the outlaw, Captain James Cook, the great explorer who sailed round the world three times in Whitby-built ships, and Count Dracula, the fictional vampire. It was in Whitby where Bram (short for Abraham) Stoker stayed while writing the supernatural Dracula story, his imagination fired by an apparently unmanned ghost ship although some say it was due to a bad dream after eating Whitby crab, the town's culinary attraction. People still visit the town in the false belief that Dracula is buried there, but remember – the dreaded Count has ne'er been seen, except upon the silver screen.

Whitby has always been a key fishing port with shell fish the most important catch. The harbour is a popular visitor attraction, yet above it on either side, red-roofed buildings rise tier upon tier and high on its headland is the moody and magnificent ruins of Whitby Abbey, its traceried frame silhouetted against the sky and hurling defiance at the restless North Sea waves. In 658, the abbey of Streoneshalh (Whitby) was founded by Oswy, King of Northumbria. This first abbey housed both men and women, and Lady Hilda (later to be Saint Hilda) was its first abbess. The waters from the abbey well, like most holy wells, were believed to be capable of curing many illnesses and Whitby became a place were people came to take the waters.

The abbey was destroyed by the Vikings in 867, rebuilt by Reinfrid in the eleventh century, and shortly after that, there's a story that Robin Hood and Little John went there to dine with the Abbot of Whitby Abbey. After they had eaten, the abbot begged them to show their prowess with the longbow; unable to refuse his request, they all went to the top of the abbey from where Robin and Little John shot an arrow each. Both arrows went over a mile and fell not far from

The view over Robin Hood's Bay.

Whitby Laths where each spot was marked with a memorial stone pillar. The locations then became known as Little John's field and Robin Hood's field. The stone pillars were still there into last century but the last I heard, both had disappeared and one had been converted into a garden roller. The abbey fell into disrepair after the Dissolution and was finally shelled by a German battle cruiser in 1914, but it still has its ghosts.

The ghosts of Whitby Abbey

Visitors to the abbey have reported seeing unusual shadows and figures. One is said to be the ghost of a nun who broke her vows and was bricked up alive. The eerie sound of a choir has been heard coming from the gaunt remains of the abbey ruins at dawn on the old Christmas Day (6 January), but the most prolific ghost is said to be St Hilda, who allegedly appears at a window overlooking the town. Other legendary tales also carry her name. Apparently when the abbey had a plague of snakes, St Hilda hurled them from the cliff and where they fell, they formed the ammonite fossils that are now found in the rocks around Whitby. People said that the sound of St Hilda's bells was so sweet they could calm storms, but the bells were stolen by pirates; the pirate's ship with the bells on board sank and now it is said that the bells ring under the deep water.

Whitby Quay with the abbey ruins on the cliff top.

St Hilda's bells also feature in another of Whitby's supernatural tales about a couple of those mythical creatures, mermaids. According to local legend, two mermaids were caught just off the coast of Whitby and imprisoned in an old shed where they were exhibited as curiosities. One evening they escaped and slipped back into the sea, but before they disappeared beneath the waves, one rose up and shouted back a curse: 'By the chimes of St Hilda's Bell, the sea shall flow to Jackdaw well'.

Despite the fact that this well was some distance inland, a few months later, a great storm lashed the coastline washing away thirteen houses and a large section of land right up to Jackdaw well. The mermaid's vengeful prophesy had been fulfilled. A more ghostly old legend states that if a sailor from Whitby died on land, on the third night after his funeral, a ghostly black coach pulled by headless horses would arrive at St Mary's graveyard. Out of the coach would troop a number of skeletal mourners, all ex-seamen, who would summon up the recently buried man and take him back with them in the black coach which plunged over the cliff into the sea.

Y28 KIRKLEES

There are numerous variations of Robin Hood's death but I've taken these lines from an old edition of *Robin Hood's Garland* when Robin declared:

> I am not able to shoot one shot more, my arrows will not flee
> But I have a cousin lives down below, please god she will bleed me.

Robin was referring to one of his kinfolk, the prioress of Kirklees Priory. Kirklees means 'church in a clearing' and lies twenty miles west of Barnsdale. When Little John and Robin arrived at the priory, the prioress feigned kindness and led Robin into an upstairs room of the priory gatehouse. There she bled him. There was nothing sinister in that; bleeding, leeching and cupping were traditional medieval treatments to cure all manner of ills:

> She blooded him in the vein of the arm and locked him up in a room
> There did he bleed all the live-long day until the next day at noon.

The spectacular ruins of
Whitby Abbey.

By this time he must have begun to suspect that some treachery was afoot and gave three weak
blasts on his horn. This brought Little John to his aid and seeing his master so close to death, he
was so distraught he was all for burning down the priory, but Robin would have none of that.
He hadn't realised that the prioress was in league with Roger of Doncaster, and between them
they had organised Robin's death:

> Sir Roger of Doncaster, by the prioress he lay
> And there they betrayed good Robin Hood through their false play.

Robin asked Little John to give him his bow and arrow and from the window, he shot an arrow
to indicate where his grave should be dug:

> Let me have length and breadth enough with a green sod under my head
> That they may say when I am dead, here lies bold Robin Hood.

ROBIN HOOD'S GRAVE
But that's part of the problem: no one now seems to know where bold Robin Hood does lie.
The accepted site is 650 yards away from the priory gatehouse where Robin purportedly shot
that last arrow, yet this would seem much too far for an arrow shot by a dying man from a
medieval longbow, which had an effective range of 250 yards.

This was confirmed by Lady Armytage, the owner of Kirklees on my recent visit. Members of the
local archery club had tested the theory and it was impossible to shoot an arrow from the gatehouse
to the site that is considered to be his grave. However, I was keen to see the site, and escorted by
Lady Armytage, it was a pleasant fifteen-minute walk from the gatehouse, along a private road,
between an avenue of trees in a well-planted and managed woodland of no great antiquity.

We reached a natural clearing canopied with swaying foliage: ahead of us was a low stone wall
bristling with high iron railings looking like some kind of cage. It is an enclosure approximately
12ft square, formed by four stone walls about 4ft high. Carved stone finials that had stood at
each corner had been smashed, half the railings had been sawn off and had either disappeared
or were bent and distorted in a display of unnecessary vandalism.

The priory gatehouse, a stone and part-timber-framed, listed building is an Elizabethan rebuild of the original monastic structure where, in an upper room, Robin Hood is traditionally thought to have breathed his last. Robin shot that legendary arrow from the window on the right.

Set in the far wall inside the enclosure is a stone tablet. It's possible to pick out odd letters yet impossible to read, but that's probably also due to the fact that it's written in some strange form of English, probably an attempt at the medieval dialect of the West Riding of Yorkshire.

Here underneath dis laitl stean	Here underneath this little stone
Laz robert earl of Huntingtun	Lies Robert Earl of Huntington
Ne'er arcir ver az hie sa geud	No archer was there as he so good
An pipl kauld im robin heud	And people call him Robin Hood
Sick utlawz as hi an iz men	Such outlaws as he and his men
Vil england niver si agen	Will England never see again

I had read that many centuries ago the grave had probably been robbed for its famous relics and the gravestone chipped away in the superstitious belief that fragments of the slab could alleviate toothache. In 1795 Joseph Ritson wrote: 'the late Sir Samuel Armytage, owner of the premises, caused the ground under it (Robin's gravestone) to be dug a yard deep and found that it had never been disturbed.' Ritson concluded that the stone had been moved from the real grave.

Sixty-five years earlier Thomas Gent in his *List of Religious Houses* told how a certain knight ordered Robin Hood's tombstone to be placed as a hearth-stone in his great hall. They experienced considerable difficulty in the transportation but eventually the stone was set. Next morning, it had mysteriously moved. Three times it was relaid yet each morning it had moved again. This obviously freaked the knight who ordered it to be taken back; did they return it to the wrong place?

To add more mystery, when the Nottinghamshire antiquarian John Throsby visited Robin Hood's Well in Nottingham in 1797, he sketched the artefacts on show. The sketches were included in the *Antiquities of Nottingham*, and there in pride of place was Robin Hood's gravestone.

By this time, Kirklees Priory had been long demolished and the estate, since 1564, was in the hands of the Armytage family, a family association that has continued for almost 500 years. The stone was used to build Kirklees Hall, now a Grade I listed building.

There are no shortage of alternative grave sites. According to Richard Grafton in his *Chronicles of 1562*, Robin was buried by the side of the main highway from Mirfield to Clipstone-upon-Calder to remind passing travellers that they could now pass without fear of being molested.

Right: The traditionally accepted version of the death scene in the upper room of the gatehouse at Kirklees Priory.

Below: The Three Nuns public house.

Researching this theory, I was directed to Dumb Steeple, a ball-topped stone pillar at the traffic island adjacent to Kirklees Park. This particular structure was built around 1760 to replace an earlier guide post that locals will tell you marked the spot of Robin's roadside grave.

A short walk from the Dumb Steeple and close to the boundary of the Kirklees estate is a public house called The Three Nuns. Vastly transformed, it's on the site of a former hostelry established after the Dissolution of the monasteries in 1539 by three nuns, Katherine Grice, Cecelia Topcliffe and Joan Laverthorpe, after their eviction from Kirklees Priory. On either side of the entrance porch, carved into the stonework is a horn and a forester's bow and quiver of arrows, the only reminder of Kirklees association with the famous outlaw.

Above: The inscription on the stone tablet inside the monument is impossible to decipher.

Right: Could the Dumb Steeple actually mark Robin's wayside grave?

Opposite below: Does the evil prioress of Kirklees haunt Robin Hood's grave?

The Ghosts of Robin Hood's Grave

Shrouded in trees and sustained by local tales of unquiet spirits, phantom prioresses and nuns that guard the grave of Robin Hood, it is easy to let the imagination run riot in a place like this. Some visitors feel an oppressive atmosphere. Many experience the sensation of being watched and one purportedly heard Robin calling Marion's name.

One day in 1926, a tenant farmer of Kirklees was shooting rabbits and rested on the wall of the grave. He was just about to shoot when he felt a tap on his shoulder: he jumped so violently, his shotgun went off, accidentally knocking two of his front teeth out on its recoil. He whirled round but there was no one to be seen.

On another occasion, this same man was on his way home from the Three Nuns Public House, taking a short cut through the Kirklees estate, when in the window of the old gatehouse he saw a man holding a bow. His family laughed and said it was the drink, yet he remained adamant that he had seen Robin Hood's ghost.

Although on private property, locals take unofficial strolls up to the grave, and one man reported seeing the figure of a woman in the white habit of a Cistercian nun emerging from some trees. Although she appeared to be solid, she made no sound, glared at him then glided silently away. He said that she conveyed intense anger and he felt that she was an evil presence, a view shared by other people who have reported seeing her.

Being there in the daylight is enough to fire the imagination, but members of the local Robin Hood Society hold unofficial night-vigils. On one occasion, one of the group became separated: when they found him, he was shaking badly and reported having just seen the figure of a woman dressed in white. Another nocturnal visitor had a terrifying experience when she saw two figures hovering in the trees beside the grave. She felt instinctively that they were the evil prioress and her paramour, Red Roger of Doncaster, who together had plotted Robin Hood's death. She said she could feel the evil emanating from them.

On another night vigil in May 2002, one of the group took a series of photographs on a Tesco disposable camera. Four of the photographs showed misty forms, one showed an orb and the others were perfectly clear. Judith Broadbent, a reporter, and her photographer colleague Sue Ellis from the *Dewsbury Reporter* were granted permission to visit the grave to cover the story. Frustratingly and for some inexplicable reason, Sue's camera jammed and she was unable to photograph the grave, but they got more than they had anticipated when Judith heard footsteps behind her and felt herself being pulled to the ground by an invisible force.

Apart from the fact that most of these people are trespassing on her land, Lady Armytage is irritated by these stories, which she considers to be grossly exaggerated, but I remain open-minded. My visit was mid-morning in the company of Lady Armytage but the day was extremely dull, the rain was incessant and under the trees the lighting very poor. Despite numerous attempts, my digital camera seemed unable to focus or register the subject, the flash didn't reach and the batteries kept playing up. In exasperation I had to accept defeat. It was only later I discovered that two of my photographs had distinctive orbs, so I have to agree with all those people – there definitely is something haunting Robin Hood's grave. Perhaps it is the remorseful prioress, or perhaps it's the great outlaw himself.

But what if Robin didn't die at Kirklees but at Kirby, a town in Nottinghamshire that sits right in the centre of Sherwood Forest? A slight mistranslation on the part of those early scribes could have turned into a mass error that has been repeated for centuries. Some historians have tried to locate his grave in the churchyard at Loxley in Staffordshire, ostensibly his ancestral home; others state he was buried in the land adjacent to Steetley Chapel in Nottinghamshire.

Another theory states that after his death, Robin's body was taken by his faithful followers to a secret location where he was buried in an unmarked grave. Throughout his life he had dodged authority by being constantly on the move, so this was perhaps the final attempt by his followers to make sure that the establishment did not discover his remains so that he could eventually rest in peace and leave us with an unending mystery.